Library Buildings, Equipment, and the ADA

Compliance Issues and Solutions

Proceedings of the
LAMA Buildings and Equipment Section Preconference,
June 24–25, 1993, New Orleans, Louisiana

Edited by
Susan E. Cirillo and Robert E. Danford

American Library Association
Chicago and London 1996

Susan E. Cirillo served as chair of the Preconference Program Planning Committee. She has been associate university librarian at the University of Massachusetts–Dartmouth, North Dartmouth, Massachusetts, since 1988.

Robert E. Danford served as moderator of the preconference. He is college librarian and director of the Stevens-German Library of Hartwick College, Oneonta, New York.

Text designed by Charles Bozett and Dianne Rooney

Composed by Publishing Services, Inc., in Goudy and Avant Garde on Xyvision/Linotype L330

Printed on 50-pound Jericho Offset Natural White, a pH-neutral stock, and bound in 10-point C1S cover stock by Victor Graphics, Inc.

The paper used in this publication meets the minimum requirements of American National Standard for Information Sciences—Permanence of Paper for Printed Library Materials, ANSI Z39.48–1992. ⊚

Library of Congress Cataloging-in-Publication Data

Library Administration and Management Association. Buildings & Equipment Section. Preconference
  (1993 : New Orleans, La.)
    Library buildings, equipment, and the ADA : compliance issues and solutions : proceedings of the LAMA
  Buildings and Equipment Section Preconference, June 24-25, 1993,
  New Orleans, Louisiana / edited by Susan E. Cirillo and Robert E. Danford.
        p.   cm.
    Includes bibliographical references and index.
    ISBN 0-8389-0673-7
    1. Libraries and the handicapped—Law and legislation—United States—Congresses. 2. United States.
  Americans with Disabilities Act of 1990—Congresses. 3. Library architecture and the physically
  handicapped—Law and legislation—United States—Congresses. 4. Library fittings and supplies—Law
  and legislation—United States—Congresses. I. Cirillo, Susan E. II. Danford, Robert E. , III. Title.
  Z679.8.L53   1993
  022′.316′63—dc20   95-40196

Printed in the United States of America

00 99 98 97 96   5 4 3 2 1

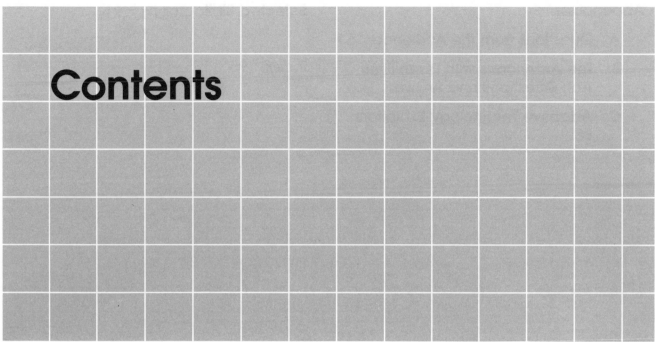

Contents

Acknowledgments   v

Introduction   vii

CHAPTER ONE
"What Do You Think You Are Doing?"   1
BARBARA PIERCE

CHAPTER TWO
The Americans with Disabilities Act   6
THOMAS M. CONTOIS

CHAPTER THREE
Issues of Building Design   14
FRED KOLFLAT AND ROBERT BRUCE KLUG

CHAPTER FOUR
Historic Properties and the ADA   19
MICHAEL HOWARD

CHAPTER FIVE
Accessible Seating for Libraries   24
ELIZABETH C. HABICH

CHAPTER SIX
Adaptive Technology   33
BARBARA T. MATES

CHAPTER SEVEN
People, Assistive Devices, ADAptive Furnishings, and Their Environment in Your Library   40
ANDREA MICHAELS AND DAVID MICHAELS

CHAPTER EIGHT
Signage and the ADA   48
CAROLYN JOHNSON

CHAPTER NINE
Safety and Security Considerations   53
RACHEL MacLACHLAN

CHAPTER TEN
The Good, the Bad, and the Ugly: Design Issues   59
FRED KOLFLAT AND ROBERT BRUCE KLUG

Appendixes

  A Questions from the Audience 63

  B The Americans with Disabilities Act: Questions and Answers 66

  C Adaptive Technology Exhibitors 88

Selected Bibliography 91
COMPILED BY BARBARA T. MATES

Index 95

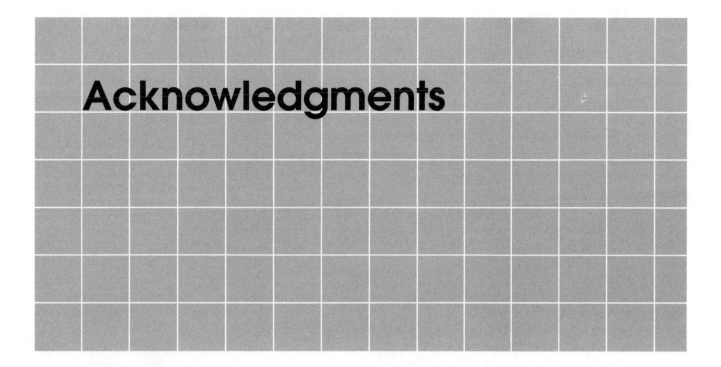

Acknowledgments

Many individuals contributed to the success of the Library Administration and Management Association (LAMA) BES preconference, "Library Buildings, Equipment, and the ADA: Compliance Issues and Solutions." The LAMA BES Safety and Security of Library Buildings Committee, then chaired by Phyllis Cutler, developed the original idea for a program on the Americans with Disabilities Act (ADA), and continued to provide support and encouragement when the broad implications of the legislation prompted its sponsorship by the Buildings and Equipment Section. The BES Executive Board and the LAMA Program Committee enthusiastically endorsed the program and encouraged its publication to a wider audience.

The Preconference Program Planning Committee was comprised of several individuals who actively demonstrated their commitment to educating librarians on accessibility issues. Robert E. Danford, Elizabeth C. Habich, Stephanie Hillman, Barbara T. Mates, Rachel MacLachlan, Andrea Michaels, David Michaels, and Larry Ostler participated in every phase of the planning process. The BES Executive Board and the BES Publications Committee encouraged publication of the proceedings and offered ongoing support. Ron Martin willingly shared his experiences in editing the proceedings of an earlier LAMA preconference.

Two individuals from the University of Massachusetts–Dartmouth deserve special recognition for their assistance in preparation of the manuscript. Heidi Silvia spent many hours transcribing audiotapes of the preconference, and Walter Frost provided his technical expertise in scanning and reproducing the graphics.

I also extend sincere appreciation to the preconference attendees who contributed to the discussion of these critical issues, and to the excellent speakers who shared their considerable knowledge and expertise.

SUSAN E. CIRILLO

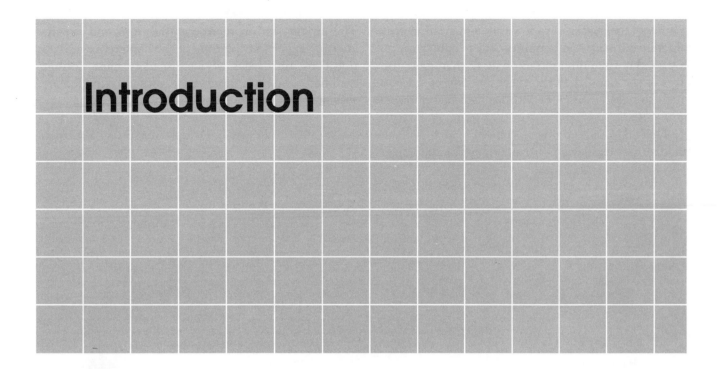

Introduction

These proceedings are the record of the presentations and deliberations of the LAMA-sponsored preconference, "Library Buildings, Equipment, and the ADA: Compliance Issues and Solutions," held June 24–25, 1993, in New Orleans, Louisiana, preceding the American Library Association's Annual Conference. This conference originated with a proposal for a program on safety and security for patrons with disabilities, submitted by the LAMA Buildings and Equipment Section, Safety and Security of Library Buildings Committee. The LAMA Program Committee recognized the need for information on the broader issues of access to library buildings, and the program was expanded to a preconference under the aegis of the Buildings and Equipment Section. This conference builds upon a very successful program held at the ALA annual meeting in San Francisco, California, in 1992, which helped introduce the library community to the concept and to the provisions of the Americans with Disabilities Act (ADA). The interest in that one program inspired the LAMA Buildings and Equipment Section to promote a program to help librarians deal with some of the most expensive and intransigent problems involved in providing library access to all citizens—the difficulties posed by bricks and mortar and architectural concepts which, in their era(s) of construction, did not take into consideration the needs of people with various physical impairments.

While it is obvious that many library buildings present barriers to those who have temporary or permanent disabilities, it is equally obvious that the members of the profession are concerned about overcoming those barriers, both to comply with the law and to comply with the goals of our profession which aspires to provide information services to all citizens who wish to make use of those services. The speakers at this conference provide useful insights to the conditions of disability, explanations of the intent and the detail of the law, and techniques for meeting the needs of library users with disabilities. But more important is the concept of common sense and good faith which permeate each of the presentations. Far more important than specific recommendations about architectural or equipment issues are the hope and confidence that people and institutions can indeed do much more than comply with the ADA; they can enhance access to information resources to an expanding audience of users. And they can do so without fear of an undue fiscal burden.

From the eloquent keynote address through the details of the law and the compliance process, and to the specifics of architectural details, equipment, signage, safety procedures, and historic preservation needs, the concepts of possibility and progress together serve to displace the fear and uncertainty which originally may have prompted people to attend the conference. Although there is still uncertainty as to the specifics of the legislation and its implementation, this conference instills the certainty that people can employ good faith and reason to do more than meet the letter of the law—they can meet *the spirit of the law*, which so neatly coincides with *the mandates of the library profession*.

The ADA is a living document which will be modified by legislation, litigation, and experience.

The articles within represent the views and experiences of experts at the time of the conference and do not constitute legal advice. Readers must consult qualified legal authority for specifics of individual issues and problems.

ROBERT E. DANFORD AND SUSAN E. CIRILLO

CHAPTER ONE

"What Do You Think You Are Doing?"

Barbara Pierce

Before I begin my prepared remarks about achieving compliance with the spirit of the Americans with Disabilities Act (ADA), I would like to call your attention to a little-known section of the ADA which sometimes looms very large for people with disabilities. It is Section 501 D—I remember it as the "501 Don't Make Me Do It" section. It appears in Title V, Construction, under the heading "Accommodations and Services." The text reads: "Nothing in this Act shall be construed to require an individual with a disability to accept an accommodation, aid, service, opportunity, or benefit which such individual chooses not to accept." In other words, disabled people are protected from having to use modifications they find to be unnecessary or inappropriate. It does not mean that a blind person can refuse to use a cassette recording of an informational brochure while continuing to demand one in Braille. But if, for example, a

library has designated a room for blind patrons to use with readers, it does protect their right to read silently in the regular reading room if they wish; it certainly protects a deaf patron from being forced to use that separate room.

Such a provision may seem self-evident, but I assure you that already disabled people have found themselves in disputes about whether or not they can be forced by providers to use modifications and programs that they do not need or want. I believe that it is important to keep this provision of the ADA in mind as we turn to an examination of what impact the Act will have on you and the library patrons you serve.

I remember vividly the tiny public library that served the small Pittsburgh suburb in which I grew up. One climbed a rickety, narrow staircase to reach it—no one who used a wheelchair could have gained entrance, since an elevator had never been contemplated. As I remember the facility, there could not have been any more than three or four rooms of books, and the children's collection must have been quite inadequate. But my elementary school library was only one very small room, and, in addition to the good books, it housed lots of encyclopedias, dictionaries, and other boring resource books; so the much larger public library was infinitely more enchanting. The librarian sat at the desk where all the library cards were filed, checked books out

Barbara Bowman Pierce is associate editor of the *Braille Monitor*, director of public education for the National Federation of the Blind, and president of the National Federation of the Blind of Ohio. She chairs the World Blind Union Committee on the Status of Blind Women, North America/Caribbean Region. As a member of the Ohio Rehabilitation Services Commission Consumer Advisory Council, she also chairs the Bureau of Services for the Visually Impaired Standing Committee. Pierce has authored numerous articles on blindness.

and in, and by her own stern decorum maintained the almost absolute silence required of everyone who dared to pass through those magical doors.

I should explain that while I was in elementary school my vision was rapidly deteriorating. I had no difficulty reading the first grade primers, but as the print shrank in size and the pictures shrank in number, I found the physical act of reading more and more difficult and less and less pleasurable. But that did not diminish my enthusiasm for good stories. My parents continued to read to me, and sometimes I could even cajole my younger brother Bobby into galloping through a chapter or two of a book—if it wasn't too full of girls.

In any case, trips to the library were eagerly anticipated and carefully planned in our family because Mother had to take us by car. She almost always came in with us to help in book selection, guiding our choices as much as her prudence and our willfulness would allow. But one fateful week my brother was sick, and my mother had to stop at the drugstore to fill a prescription for him before she came up to help me choose a book for myself and several for Bobby, who was climbing the walls of his room with boredom.

Mother had questioned me closely about whether I felt secure going into the library alone to begin choosing books. I had no doubt about my ability to see the large titles on the book spines, and I had been in the children's room so often before that the idea of having trouble never crossed my mind. But, as I realize now, in the past I had always been there with my brother or mother and the librarian had not felt any responsibility for me or concern about her collection while I was handling the books. As I entered the outermost room which contained her desk, she was dealing with another patron, so I passed unaccosted into the children's room.

It seemed to me that those shelves of books reached almost to the sky. I was sure there were more books collected in that place than I could ever manage to read, and I pined to consume them all—even the ones about cowboys or knot-tying. Looking back, I'm not sure what the attraction was. The ones I liked best had such small print and so few pictures that I could not possibly have read them, but I could enjoy the brightly colored illustrations. As I riffled through their pages, pretending to read a line or paragraph here and there, the feel and smell of the books were positively intoxicating—I don't know how long I would have been content to browse along the library shelves, picking up a book, deciphering its title, glancing through

it at the pictures, and conscientiously putting it back in the gap where it belonged.

I had never noticed how poor the lighting actually was, because always before Mother had been there to read the titles and tables of contents. Now I was struggling to read the titles for myself, but I knew she would arrive soon, and I was still having a fine time and feeling very grown-up. Then the librarian finished with the people at her desk, and she bore down on me with speed and unmistakable displeasure, even though I hadn't been making a sound and was returning the books to their exact places. With great indignation and no regard for the silence that was, according to the sign over her desk, to be maintained at all times, she demanded of me, "What do you think you are doing?"

Mercifully, time and mortification have blotted out the rest of that painful scene. My mother must have rescued me from the lecture that followed her indignant question, and we surely returned home with a supply of books, but I am absolutely certain that I never set foot in that library again. With that one question the librarian had taught me several painful lessons: (1) I was not welcome in her library or to handle her books unless my mother or little brother was there with me, (2) holding the books close to my face in order to read their titles was somehow inappropriate, and (3) my unchaperoned presence in the library was such an appalling interruption of decorum that the librarian had actually been driven to raise her voice. If other patrons had been in the library—which, thank heaven, they were not, or my humiliation would have been even more shatteringly complete—they would have heard her accusations of me. For accusations they were. To have been asked the question, "What are you doing?" would have been bad enough because it would have implied the shameful suspicion that I had been doing something detrimental to a book or to the library, which would never have occurred to me. But instead I was asked, "What do you think you are doing?" The implication was clear—in her eyes I was not actually engaged in the same activity that occupied other patrons of the library. I was pretending: these books were not for me; I did not belong.

Did that poor librarian intend to communicate all this to a small girl who was in love with books, but who could no longer read their print for herself? Probably not. She was undoubtedly uneasy at my independent appearance in her preserve and felt that she should do something, though she was not sure what. Perhaps she really was fearful that I would reshelve the books incorrectly, but, if so, I would not have been the first or last patron to do so. She clearly did not know what to do, and in her discomfort she chose an unfortunate way of articulating her willingness to help. That is the kindest construction I can place on her approach and on her question. If I am honest, however, I must admit that I am convinced there was an admixture of feeling on her part that I did not belong there—at least not without a keeper.

This incident took place more than thirty years ago and much in our society has changed during the intervening years. With varying degrees of success, we have come to recognize that community resources must be accessible to members of minority as well as majority groups. People with disabilities are only the most recent minority to win this recognition of our rights, but complete access for us has been complicated by the presence of actual physical barriers that often prevent it. If the parking is too distant, the door too heavy or too narrow, the stairs unramped, or the counter too high, actual physical access is truly and effectively denied to some people with disabilities. These obvious physical barriers are simultaneously the most difficult and easiest access problems to solve. They are difficult because solving them can be expensive, and persuading cost-conscious managers to spend money is hard these days. But they are easiest, because it is only one thing—money—that is at stake. When the appropriate modifications are made, one kind of access, genuine and measurable, has been achieved.

However, the most fundamental, insidious barriers to full participation in community life for people with disabilities are the poor attitudes about disability held by most members of the general public, including some who are disabled themselves. The bad news is that attitudes based on ignorance and misconception and shaped by fear and pity are widespread, almost ubiquitous, in society today. The good news is that, when it is possible to change these attitudes through education and exposure to sensible, competent people with disabilities, many of the access problems that seem to loom large shrink substantially or evaporate altogether.

The recently enacted civil rights legislation protecting disabled people and its implementing regulations are the subject of much discussion everywhere these days. I expect that much of the remainder of today's seminar will be spent in examining the issues raised by both the law and its regulations. But right now I wish to invite you to consider with me some ways in which attitudinal barriers, which keep disabled people out every bit as thoroughly as physical ones, can be dismantled and carted away. The first

step, it seems to me, is for those who are trying to change attitudes in themselves and others to begin gathering accurate information. We in the disability community constantly live with and struggle to resist the presumptions of others. I had never considered the point before, but I suppose I should give some credit to that librarian in Bethel Park, Pennsylvania, for bothering to ask me a question at all. Many people do not. She did not, of course, expect or wait for an answer. In fact, too frequently people presume either that disabled people have no idea what we are doing or that we think we are doing something other than what we are actually doing.

One of my favorite examples of this phenomenon has occurred repeatedly to me as I walk down the street. I live in a small town in which it is possible to walk to most places I wish to go. In fact, for years I walked to work at Oberlin College every day and popped out of my office to other places on campus for meetings and events. There is nothing tentative about the way I travel when I am walking somewhere on a schedule, yet frequently drivers pull up alongside me and, keeping pace, roll down a window to inquire, "Where are you trying to go?" Even the question, "Where are you going?" would be an intrusion on the privacy of another adult which perfect strangers would not perpetrate against any but a blind traveler. Why does the driver presume that the outcome of my trip is in doubt? Why should this information or my plans be his or her business at all? If I were hovering around a corner in obvious hesitation, looking puzzled or distressed, it would be both kind and appropriate for a stranger to inquire whether help or information would be useful. But people see what they expect to see, and, if a pedestrian is using a long white cane, in the public mind he or she is necessarily in need of rescue.

That is an example of the sort of difficulty that arises for disabled people when a person acts on a presumption which is in turn based on ignorance and misconception. We are all capable of making such mistakes and should guard against them, or at least against acting on them, by seeking accurate information and drawing sensible conclusions from the available data.

Now let us turn to the actual question of achieving access for library patrons who happen to have disabilities. Instead of asking them the question, "What do you think you are doing?" I suggest that you ask this question of yourselves. Are you attempting merely to comply with federal regulations? If so, your job is at least clear-cut. There are rules to follow and specifications to meet. Once you have done that, your job is complete. You will be safe from lawsuits, but don't be surprised if your facility does not attract many of the people for whom the modifications were made. They will soon discover that, though the physical barriers are gone, the attitudinal ones are intact.

But if, as I hope and believe, your true goal is to make disabled people genuinely welcome in your library, your efforts to comply with the Americans with Disabilities Act will not stop with removing the physical barriers. A broader vision of equal access is what advocates of the ADA had in mind when they worked for its passage. And where better, more appropriate for this broader concept to take root than in the nation's libraries? Libraries are still the jumping-off point for people with hopes and dreams, the repositories of our understanding of freedom and justice. And who better to set the equal-access agenda in the months and years ahead than librarians, the keepers of that flame?

The physical requirements of the ADA can be learned and implemented, but beneath (or perhaps beyond) the regulations lie common sense and good-will: the intention to achieve equality. Whether we will look back on this decade and admit that institutions of various kinds settled for complying with the letter of the Americans with Disabilities Act, or will say with pride that they embraced its spirit, will depend on people like you.

Obviously, I hope that people in positions of responsibility will take this opportunity to encourage a change in attitude: their own, their colleagues', the public's, and that of disabled people. A good beginning place is to help library staff members become more comfortable in the presence of people with disabilities. You might invite people in your community who have disabilities of various kinds to form an advisory committee, temporary or permanent, depending on the complexity of your program. Bring them and the staff together to discuss constructive modifications, changes that members of the disabled community recognize as important or necessary and that are possible to undertake. Committee members can also do inservice training for library staff members. Many of the things your colleagues do not know are painfully obvious to would-be patrons with disabilities.

> A person seated in a wheelchair cannot conveniently check out a book at a high desk, but the desk doesn't have to be replaced immediately; just place a table and chair beside it so the staff member on duty can sit down and be at the same level as the seated patron.

Because there are many degrees of vision loss, patrons may well be capable of using the large-print collection and certainly can use the commercially recorded cassette book and music collections without being able to spot and read library signs, even the large-print ones now mandated by the ADA. Inquiries by these patrons should not be answered with vague gestures, or directions like, "over there behind the woman in the green sweater." Learning to give helpful directions takes a little practice, but it is not hard once staff members get over the panic of realizing that the person facing them cannot necessarily see the usual landmarks.

No one in the disability community expects people to know instinctively what is appropriate, even necessary. We are well used to articulating our requirements and preferences. There are as many differences among us and our abilities as there are in any other cross-section of society. We do not expect you and your staff to read minds, but it would be very helpful if you could persuade library personnel to ask questions when they are not certain what to do. Actually, that part is not particularly difficult; it's the second step that's tough—getting them to listen to the answers and be guided by them. It is frustrating (and embarrassing to both parties) to ask for directions to a public telephone and in response be dragged to the ladies' room.

Ideally the aim should be to treat disabled adults as adults until and unless by their behavior they indicate that more custodial treatment is appropriate. If a person using a white cane enters your library and asks for directions to the reference desk, simply provide the information requested—that's what you would do for a sighted patron. If the person seems uncertain and if you or someone else is free to do so, you might offer to accompany him or her. But if the person says that the instructions are clear and starts in the correct direction, you should not insist on walking along or following to see that nothing happens. There is no reason to call the reference desk to warn your colleague to watch for a blind person. I can assure you that there are few things more unnerving than trying to follow a set of directions while someone is trailing along behind, gasping every time the long cane touches an object, and grabbing at one's arm or waist every time the observer fears that something may go wrong.

By the same token, you should not put up with behavior from a disabled patron that you would find unacceptable from an able-bodied one. Let me be clear. Under some circumstances modifications of library policy should be worked out if possible, in order to make a particular collection available to a disabled patron. For example, a blind person with a reader will necessarily make a little noise in reading the material that must be used in the building. It would be considerate to everyone to assign the pair a distant corner or small room for reading. Likewise, it may be necessary to rearrange the chairs at a table in order for a person who uses a wheelchair to work there in comfort. But it is not reasonable for a blind patron to expect that a librarian can stop his or her assigned tasks to provide extended reading services. The test is, how much time would the librarian spend assisting another patron who needed help?

It is reasonable and appropriate to refuse to provide some kinds of assistance even when the refusal results in inconvenience to the disabled person. No one gains anything in the long run if people with disabilities are encouraged to take advantage of other people's goodwill or sense of pity simply because of a disability. Assistance-dog users, for example, should be required to keep their animals close to them and under control. Dogs should not be allowed to sprawl in the aisle, forcing other patrons to step over or around them. It is also inappropriate for dog users to ask others to take their dogs outdoors to a relief area.

It is easy for me to stand here and tell you that there are times when it's appropriate for your staff to bend established rules and times when it isn't necessary to do so. But people find it hard to distinguish between such situations unless they have the opportunity to discuss these matters with sensible disabled people. So I come back to the concept of the advisory committee. Not only will you begin to understand the difference between appropriate services resulting from an effort to provide reasonable accommodation and those being requested by disabled people who have done poor planning or who are simply self-indulgent, but you will also find yourself with an excellent conduit for spreading the word among disabled people that the library staff are genuinely trying to make all patrons feel welcome to use this community resource.

All this will take time. We have been kept "down and out" for a number of years. The message that we were not welcome was clearly given and was just as clearly received. Habits of thought and patterns of action take time to change.

"What do you think you are doing?" If you are making room for everyone in your community who wants to use the library, regardless of disability, you can succeed. It will require everyone, staff and patrons alike, to change some attitudes. Broadening horizons and expanding awareness always require such adjustments. But surely the results are worth the effort.

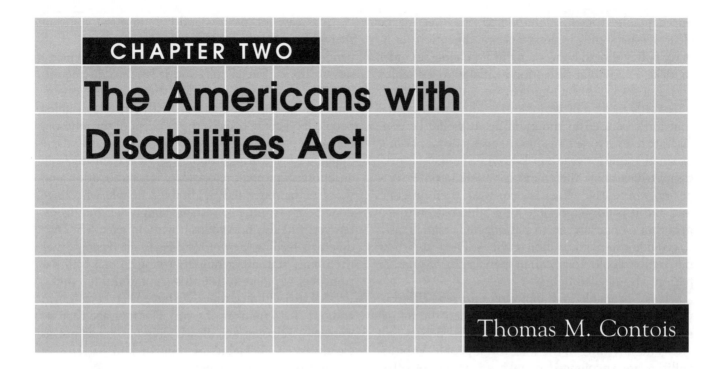

CHAPTER TWO

The Americans with Disabilities Act

Thomas M. Contois

I am a trial attorney in the Public Access Section of the Civil Rights Division, Department of Justice (formerly the Office on the ADA), which has enforcement responsibilities for Titles II and III of the ADA. In addition, our purpose is to educate the public, the people who have both rights and responsibilities under the ADA. Our goal is to encourage voluntary compliance and to disseminate accurate information.

Before I continue, I will reiterate some of Barbara Pierce's advice. She provided excellent suggestions for things that are very easily done—both to provide greater access to facilities and services and to comply with the law. Examples are providing a table near the checkout counter where a staff member can sit on the same level with someone who uses a wheelchair, or rearranging tables and chairs in a reading room (or at a carrel) so that someone who uses a wheelchair can more easily gain access to those areas. Or, in making

a slight modification in a policy, to allow a person who's blind and who comes in with a reader to be able to use your services. A variety of easily accomplished adjustments will satisfy 90 or 95 percent of compliance with the letter of the law.

Another suggestion that I will repeat is to seek advice from people with disabilities. Setting up a committee to provide that input is a very good suggestion. People with disabilities live with their disabilities every day and know what they need and know what other people who are similarly situated need. They will provide you with insights and information that you won't get otherwise, and will make you think about things that would not have occurred to you. In part, I want to reassure you that complying with the law is probably not as difficult as you may have been told.

The Structure of the Act

Title I

The ADA is organized into five titles, or sections, each dealing with a different topic. Title I of the ADA covers employment provisions. It applies to private companies and governs the way that they deal with their employees. In sum, it prohibits discrimination on the basis of

Thomas M. Contois received his A.B. from Duke University in 1986 and his J.D. from Duke University School of Law in 1990. He began working as a trial attorney in the Civil Rights Division of the Department of Justice in September 1992. During his tenure in the Civil Rights Division he has worked exclusively on matters arising under Titles II and III of the ADA and Section 504 of the Rehabilitation Act.

disability. If you have applicants with disabilities who are qualified to do a job, you can't refuse them the job simply because they have a disability. In other words, they must have the same opportunities for being hired and for receiving promotions, and must receive the same pay and the same benefits—all the terms and conditions of employment should be the same.

Perhaps the most significant provision of Title I is the one that requires employers to make "reasonable accommodations" for people with disabilities. This requirement applies when an applicant qualified for the essential functions of a job is prevented by a disability from doing either some non-essential functions, or from being able to do the essential functions of the job unless the employer makes some change in the way the job is done. For example, someone who has paraplegia and uses a wheelchair applies for a typist's position, types 90 wpm error-free and is well qualified for the job, but his or her wheelchair is too large to fit under the employer's computer desks. That is not a reason to refuse to hire the person. It would be a reasonable accommodation for the employer to do any number of things to allow that person to do the job. The easiest would be to put the desk up on a pair of blocks to make it high enough for the wheelchair. Or it may be a reasonable accommodation to replace the desk. Or it is a reasonable accommodation to let that person work at home if it is the kind of work they can do at home without creating other problems. Obviously there are some situations that are more difficult to handle, but most of them can be as easily resolved.

Title I is enforced by the Equal Employment Opportunity Commission (EEOC), an independent federal agency with responsibility for enforcing a variety of federal civil rights laws. If you have questions about Title I, contact them at (800) 669-EEOC. They are the experts on Title I much more so than the staff in the Public Access Section.

Title II

Title II applies to state and local governments and the facilities, programs, and services that they provide. The basic requirement under Title II is to provide "program access." That means when evaluating a state or local program or service, the program or service is viewed in its entirety. In its entirety it must be as accessible to people with disabilities as it is to people without disabilities.

I will give an example of how this might work. Suppose a county is offering tax assistance to residents

and it provides some informational material about tax returns. In addition to the printed material, there may also be tax preparers who would give advice on how to fill out tax forms. The county provides this service at its main public library and also at its four branch libraries. The program as a whole must be accessible to people with disabilities. That doesn't necessarily mean that every one of the branches and the main library must be accessible. If, for instance, four out of the five were accessible to people who used wheelchairs, that might be sufficient to qualify for program access. If the fifth library were not accessible, you would not be required to undergo major architectural renovations in order to make that building accessible, as long as there are other locations that are accessible. Or, if, instead of using the inaccessible libraries you could use other county buildings that were accessible and relocate the program, you could deal with it that way.

The bottom line is that you have a great deal of flexibility in deciding how to provide program access. That is the good news. The not-so-good news is that you absolutely have to do it, unless it places an undue financial or administrative burden on you—a very difficult standard to meet. In its interpretation, it means that it is extremely difficult or extremely expensive—and so far we haven't encountered many examples of situations that qualify for that. So you must comply, but you do have some flexibility in achieving the solution.

There are also some other specific provisions that I will mention briefly. For instance, there is the provision on providing auxiliary aids and services—a variety of things that would enable people with hearing, vision, or speech impairments to gain access to your materials. They include, for instance, qualified sign language interpreters. They also include providing materials in alternative formats, either in Braille or audiotape. If you have materials on videotape, providing a transcript or captioning it may be necessary. In other words, there are a variety of choices that you can make to fulfill the requirement, but you must provide auxiliary aids and services when it is necessary to allow a person with a disability to participate in the program or service.

In addition, there is also the requirement to make reasonable modifications in policies and practices when that is necessary to allow a person with a disability to participate in the program. And this you must do unless it is a fundamental alteration of the program.

I will give two examples, one that is a fundamental alteration and one that is not.

As an example of something that might be a fundamental alteration of a program, suppose, in a tour of a cave, part of the tour consisted of turning out all the lights to demonstrate abject blackness, the impenetrable darkness. And on the tour a person who is deaf and has a sign language interpreter requests that you leave the lights on during that part of the tour, in order to continue to see the interpreter. That might well be a fundamental alteration of that part of the tour, and you might not be required to do that because the whole idea is to have the blackness, and having the light on would ruin the experience. (As you can see, that is a contrived example, but that is almost how far you must go to be excused from the provision of making reasonable modifications.)

An example that is not a fundamental alteration will be very similar to the example that Barbara Pierce (*see* Chapter 1) offered, about the blind person who comes into the library with a reader. Obviously there is a policy that people must be quiet, that you can't read aloud, and it would be a reasonable modification of that policy to allow the reader to read in some part of the reading room or some place in the library where it would not disturb other people. Similarly, you might have a policy, particularly in a university library, that restricts the use of closed carrels. It would be a reasonable modification of that policy to allow someone with a disability to use a closed carrel even if they didn't meet the standard criteria, because that would enable them to use a reader they were not able to use in the main reading room.

Finally, Title II sets architectural standards for new construction and for alterations. When building a new building or altering an existing building, you can choose to comply with either the Uniform Federal Accessibility Standards (UFAS) or the new ADA Accessibility Guidelines (ADAAG). The Uniform Federal Accessibility Standards have been in effect for a number of years—they are the accessibility standards that applied under the Rehabilitation Act of 1973 and as they were amended in 1978. Recipients of federal funding have been covered by that act, and new buildings since 1978 have been required to comply with UFAS.

Title III

Title III applies to private businesses; it doesn't govern their relationships with their employees but rather with their customers. Its provisions are somewhat similar to those of Title II, although there are a few differences. I will cover the requirements that are most applicable to libraries. There is, again, the provision requiring reasonable modification of policies and procedures, and also the same provision on auxiliary aids and services. The architectural provisions are generally the same with respect to new construction and alterations. Under Title III, however, you don't choose which set of standards to follow; you must follow the ADA Accessibility Guidelines.

The real difference between Titles II and III is with respect to existing facilities. As I mentioned earlier, Title II's central requirement is program access. You might not be required to actually make the facility accessible in order to comply with program access—you could move the programs to another location or develop an alternative solution that would relieve you of the responsibility of actually making architectural changes. That is not the case under Title III.

Under Title III, when you're a privately owned (or operated) place of public accommodation, like a library, your obligation in your existing facilities is to remove architectural barriers to access where it's readily achievable to do so. By "readily achievable" we mean things that you can do that are not very expensive. It generally does not mean adding an elevator, for instance, to a three-story building that has only stairs. It does mean providing a ramp in place of steps at the entrance, or widening doors, or making changes in restrooms to make them more accessible. And you must make all the changes that are readily achievable; it doesn't matter that you may have another facility someplace else that is accessible and people can get everything there that they can get at the inaccessible location. Under Title III, you must make changes to every facility where it is readily achievable to do so.

There are some differences in the way that Titles II and III are enforced. Titles II and III are both enforced by the Department of Justice. Title III is enforced exclusively by the Public Access Section, while Title II is also enforced by other agencies of the Civil Rights Division. In general, Title II complaints are originally received by the Department of Justice, but some of them are farmed out to other agencies. For instance, complaints that deal with public schools, whether they're elementary, secondary, or postsecondary, are referred to the Department of Education, which has had enforcement responsibility under the Rehabilitation Act for a number of years. Since virtually every public school in the country receives some federal financial assistance, the Department of Education has taken on the Title II responsibility in addition to the Rehabilitation Act responsibilities. And their enforcement, of course, is decentralized under different regions. You may be familiar with the Office of Civil Rights in your region—they have the Title II responsibility for your library.

Titles IV and V

There are two other titles of the ADA. Title IV requires every state to have had in place by July 26, 1993, a telecommunications relay system. This is a system that allows people with hearing or speech impediments to use a Telecommunications Device for Deaf Persons (TDD) to make phone calls to people who don't have TDDs. Basically, you call the relay operator who has the TDD and either the operator or the person who calls can have a TDD conversation. The operator then relays the conversation word-for-word. If you want to call somebody with a TDD and you don't have one, you can call the relay service and they'll use the TDD to call the TDD user. The Federal Communications Commission (FCC) enforces Title IV.

Title V covers miscellaneous provisions that are important but difficult to characterize as a group. It includes enforcement provisions and the provision on not requiring anyone to accept an accommodation or modification that he or she doesn't wish to accept. Provisions dealing with insurance companies—which are generally exempted from federal legislation—and a variety of other things are included.

Technical Assistance Efforts

Finally, I will discuss what the Department of Justice has been doing with respect to Titles II and III. In addition to our enforcement effort, we have a statutorily mandated technical assistance effort. Congress recognized the need to educate the public about rights and responsibilities under the ADA. They also understood that education would be the best way to promote voluntary compliance. That technical assistance effort is coordinated by the Public Access Section.

There are four major parts of our technical assistance effort. First, we've authored a number of publications that provide information about the ADA. We have a booklet with a variety of commonly asked questions and answers about all titles of the ADA. We also have technical assistance manuals for both Titles II and III which are attempts to explain clearly the require-

ments in layman's terms. The EEOC has published a technical assistance manual for Title I, and you can request a copy by calling their toll-free number, below.

The second part of our technical assistance effort is a speakers' bureau, through which our staff is available to speak to organizations that want to know more about the ADA.

The third part is our twenty-four hour telephone line; an automated answering system is available around the clock. In addition, the telephone line is staffed by the Public Access Section from 11:00 a.m. to 5:00 p.m., EST, Monday through Friday. If you have questions about Title I, you should call the EEOC. The EEOC line is both voice and TDD (we have separate voice and TDD lines). Our voice number is (800) 514-0301. Our TDD line is (800) 514-0383.

Finally, the fourth part of our technical assistance effort is a grant program. In 1991 we awarded about $3.5 million in grants to nineteen trade organizations and disability rights groups. They in turn provided informational materials, seminars, training sessions or telephone assistance for their members or the general public. We are about to award another $2.5 million in grants to between ten and fifteen recipient organizations. Again, it will probably be a mix of both trade groups and disability rights groups.

Enforcement of Titles II and III

Enforcement of Titles II and III proceeds roughly the same way. We receive complaints from members of the general public. We investigate those by getting whatever information we can from the person who files the complaint and talking to the respondent, the person who's alleged to be in violation. Frequently the investigation will involve a visit to the facility so that we can assess the problems and determine potential solutions. After we've gathered the information we try to negotiate a solution. If we can't reach a solution in that informal negotiating process, the case will be referred to litigation.

At this point, the Department of Justice has brought two lawsuits under Title III. We are participating in a few more under both Titles II and III. We've received approximately 1,400 complaints under Title II. About half have been retained by the Department of Justice for investigation; the others have been referred to other agencies. We've also received roughly 1,400 complaints under Title III. We've opened about 1,100 of those for investigation by our office, and there are about 800 currently under investigation.

The first case that the Department of Justice filed under Title III is *United States* v. *Becker CPA Review*, a case involving auxiliary aids and services. The Becker CPA Review, headquartered in California, provides review courses for people preparing to take the CPA exam. They teach approximately 10,000 students annually. We received complaints from two students who are deaf. A tape-recorded instructional session was played by a CPA and Becker had agreed to provide a transcript for the deaf students. Unfortunately, the CPA who played the tape didn't just play the tape; he would frequently press the "stop" button and add comments contradicting the tape, and would also take questions from the students. The first few times that one of our complainants attended, his wife went with him and interpreted. He counted dozens of times when there was a departure from the transcript. We felt that the transcript was not an adequate auxiliary aid and service. Becker refused to provide anything else and we couldn't get it resolved. So that situation led to a lawsuit, and it's still in litigation.

The second lawsuit we filed was against the Venture department stores. This chain of discount department stores had a policy requiring a driver's license to accept payment by check. For most people that's not a problem, but for individuals whose disabilities prevent them from driving, that can be a very difficult problem. All states issue photo identification cards which resemble driver's licenses, have a photograph, have all the same information as driver's licenses, but don't entitle the holder to drive. We had four complainants who had state photo identification cards, who had various disabilities that meant they couldn't drive, and they challenged Venture's policy. We were able to resolve the case on the same day that we filed, actually by prearrangement with Venture. We entered a consent decree and Venture agreed to accept state photo identification cards as legitimate identification for check-cashing purposes. We expect that retail outlets all over the country will now be changing their policies for check cashing.

There are a few other lawsuits that we are participating in, including *Galloway* v. *the District of Columbia*. Galloway was excluded from jury service simply because he was blind. He challenged this under Title II. The federal District Court for the District of Columbia found in his favor and said that we have blind attorneys, that we have blind witnesses, and that there are a lot of people in the courtroom who are blind, and they get along fine. So there is no basis upon which to say that somebody who is blind can't serve

on a jury for that reason alone. The district's policy of not even allowing blind jurors to be considered for jury duty was a violation of Title II. At that point the proceedings were paused and the question now is whether Mr. Galloway is entitled to any damages for having been excluded. The federal judge asked the Department of Justice to give its views on that question. We did feel that he was entitled to damages and have filed a brief to that effect.

A case in California has been filed by a private litigant against one of the International House of Pancakes franchises in San Diego. It's a barrier removal case—removing architectural barriers and also providing auxiliary aids, i.e., menus in alternative formats in Braille or on tape. The defendant's primary defense in arguing that it violates the United States Constitution is a challenge to the constitutionality of the ADA. Whenever that happens the judge is required by federal statute to give notice to the Attorney General of the United States that the constitutionality of a federal statute has been challenged. The Attorney General can defend the statute if she chooses. We're doing that now.

Finally, you may be familiar with a case undergoing appeal now. The city of Philadelphia, in resurfacing its streets, did not provide curb cuts at the corners to allow access for people with mobility impairments, particularly those using wheelchairs. The plaintiffs argued that the resurfacing of the streets constituted an alteration under Title II. As such they had to be made accessible and that included providing the curb cuts. The federal court agreed. The city is appealing that ruling and the Department of Justice is filing an *amicus curiae* (friend of the court) brief, in the Third Circuit Court of Appeals.

That summarizes what has happened so far. Rather than address examples (we have hundreds), a better use of our time may be to respond to questions.

Questions from the Audience

Is a public library in an existing building required to renovate to conform with ADAAG within three years?

Not necessarily. Under Title II there's a requirement that every state and local government entity conduct a self-evaluation of all its services, programs, and facilities to identify problems—barriers to access. At the same time, you must develop a transition plan detailing how you will solve these problems. The deadline in the regulations is three years from the effective date of the act, which will be in 1995. Any physical changes that are required under the transition plan must be completed by then. It may be, however, that no physical changes are required for particular buildings because they may already be accessible enough, or there are no programs in that building that need to be accessible or that can't be moved to another building. That is, you are not required to retrofit to comply with ADAAG or UFAS unless it is necessary to meet the program access requirement.

I'm working in safety and security and there are many relatively inexpensive security equipment options, like visible and audible alarm systems. Are those the types of things that by 1995 we should have in place?

Yes. But, of course, their installation won't necessarily mean that you come up to full compliance with either UFAS or ADAAG in an existing facility. It's often very difficult to go back and retrofit an existing facility to make it fully compliant with either UFAS or ADAAG. There are some facilities where it can be done without too much difficulty, but in others it can be very difficult and very expensive. Congress was aware of that, and that's why under Title III you're only required to do what's readily achievable with the existing facilities. You're not required to go back and retrofit your existing facilities to make them fully accessible. It would be too difficult and too expensive and you could go bankrupt trying to do it. The trade-off was that from this point forward, everything that we build will be fully accessible to, and usable by, people with disabilities. So there are much stricter standards for new construction and for alterations, additions, or renovations to existing facilities. But if it's just in existing facilities, you generally don't have to go back and retrofit it to bring it up to full compliance.

If a municipal library, with a total budget of $50,000, was not accessible (two stories, no elevator, fifteen stairs up to the building), and the self-evaluation determined that the cost would be prohibitive, would it be exempt?

I have a two-part answer. First, the only excuse that you have for not making the program accessible is if it's an undue financial or administrative burden. I will give an example of how someone might argue that it would not be an undue financial or administrative burden for you to provide an accessible library facility. It is certainly within the power of the mu-

nicipality to find some additional source of revenue (through a bond issue or a tax increase, for example) to generate revenue to provide access to the facility. It is certainly conceivable that a private litigant could take a position like that, or that the Department of Justice could take a position like that (I'm not saying the Department of Justice would take this position or that we have), and a court could agree with it. They could say that the fact that you don't have money in the current budget isn't good enough, because the money is there—you just have to collect it from the members of the community. In other words, an exemption from this standard may be very, very difficult to achieve.

Second, you may be able to accomplish program access without making that building accessible, if you provide, for instance, a mail or mobile book lending service that would provide everything that is in the building. You could provide alternative forms of service that might meet your obligations.

I suppose it would be a problem if you had a meeting room in that building?

Yes, unless you make another meeting room in an accessible building available on the same basis and in roughly the same geographical location. In other words, if you've got one at one end of the county and another at the other end of the county, it's not going to be good enough if one is accessible and the other is not. But again, the service of providing the meeting room can be provided in another facility if that's the way that you want to do it, but the question is going to be whether you can really do it. The idea is to make sure that things are as equal as possible so that people with disabilities can have as much access to the meeting room of the library as people without disabilities. Frequently you have a complex of municipal buildings and it makes very little difference whether the meeting is in building A or building B. But if you don't have an alternate, accessible facility, it may be a tougher question.

You mentioned providing bookmobile or curb services as an alternative service. What if your bookmobile is your service in rural communities? Does that unit have to be wheelchair accessible, or are people expected to come to the main library or to a branch that might be accessible?

The interior of the vehicle may not need to be accessible but the service that the bookmobile provides must be as accessible to people with disabilities as it is to people without disabilities. If that means that you have to bring material out of the vehicle down to the curb or sidewalk, then that would be the way that you could make the bookmobile accessible. It would not be acceptable to say that someone with a disability must go to the main library to get that material. At that point the bookmobile service is not accessible to people with disabilities and that's not program access.

Is an association library that receives about 70 percent of its funding from the town, but is governed by a private board, covered under Title III or under Title II?

It is possible to have, with respect to one facility, two different sets of obligations. The Title II entities, the state or the local governments, will have the Title II obligations with respect to that facility and its operation. The Title III entities will have Title III obligations with respect to that entity. Title II entities never have Title III obligations and vice versa, but they can have independent sets of obligations existing simultaneously. In cases like that, the Title II entity that is funding this service has to make sure that it meets the program access requirement. In addition, the Title III entity has obligations to provide auxiliary aids and services, to remove barriers where it's readily achievable, to make reasonable modifications in its policies and practices, and so on, so that it doesn't violate Title III. In that situation, both titles come into play.

So, in other words, in the example of a library that is not accessible, an association library with only private funding would only have to worry about making it accessible if it were financially feasible?

The Title III entity only has to do what's readily achievable with respect to the architectural barriers. The Title II entity must provide program access unless it constitutes an undue financial or administrative burden. That might mean architectural work or relocating the program, or it might mean some alternative forms of service, such as curb-side service or home delivery or mail service. (It may be hard to establish that it's going to be an undue financial burden on the Title II entity.)

If a public library leases a building which was built for its exclusive use by a private enterprise before the ADA, and there is no language in the lease agreement addressing who might be responsible for mandated building changes, who would be responsible for those changes—the owner, the lessor, or the lessee?

Under Title III, the responsible entities are not just the owners of facilities, but also anyone who operates a place of public accommodation, and anyone who leases all or part of a place of public accommodation. For instance, in a mall, the owner of the mall, the management company that operates it, and every one of the tenants would be responsible for removing architectural barriers to access.

When deciding what was readily achievable we would look at the resources of all of those people combined. It doesn't matter what the lease says. The parties can work it out and decide who's going to pay for it if they want to do that. If it were to go to a lawsuit, all of them would be defendants and they all would be responsible. It's up to them to figure out who's going to pay for compliance.

In the situation that you've described where one of the entities is a Title II entity, we're back to the situation that we discussed a few minutes ago. The Title III entity has the Title III obligations; the Title II entity that is operating there as a lessor does not have Title III responsibilities. A Title II entity never has Title III responsibilities but it does have all of the program access requirements that apply under Title II.

Is a private college (as opposed to a state university or a state-operated college) a Title III or a Title II entity?

If it's private, it can only be a Title III entity. Private, as opposed to public, is the distinction between III and II. A private college would be considered a place of public accommodation. One of the twelve categories of places of public accommodation under Title III is "places of education." It would include private colleges, private secondary schools, private kindergartens, and day care centers, which would all be covered under Title III.

In the design of barrier-free buildings we currently function under three different requirements in the design process: ADA compliance, the building code compliance—Building Officials Conference of America (BOCA) or Southern Building Congress, and the state requirements. Often they're in conflict. In many cases the states are far more restrictive. It is my understanding that there was to be an agreement or a document that would establish the requirements, and that they would be accepted by BOCA and the other codes. Would you comment on that situation?

Frequently there are disparate provisions between a state or a local code and the requirements of the ADA. There is a process by which, over time, the situation can be resolved. There is a certification provision in the ADA that enables any authority that has a building code, whether state or local government, to submit the building code to the state's attorney general for review. If the code is certified as complying with the ADA, any building that is built in conformance to that code is then assumed to be in compliance with the ADA. Should they ever be sued, it's not a complete defense but it's a strong defense.

There are roughly 3,000 building code authorities around the country, so it will be some time before all the codes are submitted and approved. The first one came from the state of Washington and the Department of Justice recently told Washington that it's not good enough. It's a very exacting review. We hope that twenty years from now these problems will be resolved. I realize that's not much help right now, but at least that's the way it's supposed to be solved in the long run.

If you have additional questions about either Title II or III, and would like an official written answer from the Department of Justice, write to:

Mr. John L. Wodatch
Public Access Section
Civil Rights Division
U.S. Department of Justice
P.O. Box 66738
Washington, DC 20035-6738

Update on Status of Litigation, June 1994

In the time since the LAMA preconference in June 1993, there have been some developments in the litigation I discussed. First, the Becker case was settled in May 1994. Becker agreed to change its policy to provide sign language interpreters for students who need them. In addition, Becker paid $20,000 to the United States, to be distributed to students with disabilities who had been discriminated against, and agreed to establish a $25,000 scholarship for students with hearing impairments at California State University – Northridge.

Second, the Galloway case has been decided. The United States District Court for the District of Columbia found that Mr. Galloway was entitled to recover compensatory damages under Title II of the ADA, and awarded him $30,000. In the International House of Pancakes case in California, the district court ruled that the ADA is constitutional, and that matter is going forward. Finally, the Third Circuit Court of Appeals has ruled in *Kinney* v. *Yerusalem* (the case concerning Philadelphia's resurfacing of streets) that the district court was correct in finding that the city had violated Title II when it failed to provide curb cuts.

In addition, since June 1993 the Department of Justice has filed more lawsuits under Title II of the ADA. These include lawsuits against two dentists, one in Houston and one in New Orleans, for refusing to treat patients who were HIV-positive. The Department has also filed a friend of the court brief in a case pending in the United States District Court for the District of Massachusetts (in Boston), brought by a private plaintiff against Boston University. Her lawsuit alleges that the university denied her application for admission to its school of social work because she has Tourette's syndrome.

The Department has received several hundred more complaints under both Titles II and III, and continues to investigate those matters. To ensure compliance, the Department anticipates filing several more lawsuits in the coming months.

CHAPTER THREE
Issues of Building Design

Fred Kolflat and Robert Bruce Klug

In many states the ADA is just one part of the requirements for providing accessibility. In Texas, for example, there are many components of the Texas Elimination of Architectural Barriers Act that are more stringent than ADAAG. There are actually two mistresses to be served—the federal government and the state. In the state of Texas we are very concerned about the state standards because they are more visible to us and because we must submit documentation of compliance.

Another point I want to emphasize is to keep your sights high. Compliance with ADAAG or state codes is just part of the challenge that you have as fellow designers of your building, whether it relates to new construction or to bringing an existing building into compliance. You should not lose sight of the need to continue to provide creative design solutions for the

Fred Kolflat, a partner in the architecture firm of Budd Beets Harden Kolflat, has long been involved in building accessibility issues. He designed a state-of-the-art accessible building in Austin which houses the Texas Rehabilitation Commission.

Robert Bruce (R. B.) Klug, AIA, is a partner/architect at Klug & Boerner Architects & Planners in Austin, Texas. He has over twenty years' experience in architecture and construction, including management of large ($100+ million) projects and additions to local library structures. Klug has conducted accessibility audits for organizations as large as the University of Texas–Austin.

functions of a library. As a former employer used to say, "If you want to get to the harbor just over the horizon, don't aim at the horizon, aim higher up, set your sights higher."

So, let us think of ADAAG as but one component in the overall design process. We are constantly learning about compliance and how it can relate to good quality design. There are creative ways to infuse excitement into your projects—both to comply with ADAAG and to be a showcase for some new ideas.

Let me assure you that ADAAG is here to stay. It will be improved, with time, through trial and error. No pun intended with the trial, but that's bound to happen. Information on the guidelines is available through the U. S. Department of Justice. The American Institute of Architects (AIA) in Washington has a synopsis that is easier to read than the Act itself. For those of you who are involved with renovating an existing facility, the Building Owners and Managers Association (BOMA) International has a checklist on renovation that can be very helpful.

There are not very many library-specific design restraints imposed by ADAAG. As examples, one checkout lane must be accessible; security gates and turnstiles must comply; card catalogs and magazine racks must comply with the reach range criteria; there is a minimum requirement of three feet between ranges, but there is no limit to the number of shelves; and at least 5 percent of the user seating must comply.

There are a few examples of buildings that have been designed not only to comply but also to lead the way. I will use a building in Austin, Texas, as an example. It's a large building with a large parking structure on a very steep site, and yet there are no steps. A series of ramps has been provided to accommodate those who are not able to walk easily. There is a walking trail that was designed to allow people in some of the neighboring buildings which serve the blind, to walk on a variety of surfaces and to become accustomed to the feel and sound of different surfaces. It's an interesting idea. Imagine yourself as not being sighted; your ears become an extremely important extension of your mind and your body. The ability to practice using other senses was thought to be important enough to be a part of the design. Covered parking is provided for people with disabilities—not just parking at the top level, but prime parking space readily accessible to the building.

The entry court has colored and very textured paving materials and it is without curb edges. The court has ceramic buttons that a cane can feel, to allow those who are without sight to find their way to the front of the building. All signage is in Braille, not just mandated signage. Behind the elevator banks on every floor, there is a specially enclosed vestibule that is fire protected. During an emergency, someone in a wheelchair can be safe within this area. Unlike typical elevators that return to the first floor during a fire and then are accessible only to the Fire Chief, these elevators are available to those in wheelchairs to provide egress to a safe environment.

In this building the restroom entrances are curved corridors, acoustically treated to prevent sound within the toilet area from coming out to the hallway, but there are no doors. Usually you go through two doors and, if you time it right, you can actually pass through the first one in a wheelchair before you get swacked and then you go through the second one. In this case, someone can move from the hallway into the toilet areas without passing through a door.

The light fixtures and the power outlets are at a convenient height throughout the building so that, whether you're seated in a wheelchair or standing, you can have easy access to the light switches. In the auditorium, various levels of ramp allow access from the main level to the speaker's rostrum or, in fact, to any room on the floor. The provision is to allow easy access throughout this whole ensemble. In the dining area,

glass is lower than usual to accommodate those who are seated. The intent is to integrate the responses to ADAAG (and to state codes) without becoming blatantly obvious—to integrate the whole into a universal design.

These are just a few examples of opportunities that you can find in projects with your architect. I encourage you to seek new ways to solve these problems and to go beyond them because ADAAG is only part of a larger picture. Try to think through the way in which a person with a disability would use your facility. If you had a disability, what would you want to see, what would you want to hear, what would you want to experience?

Existing Buildings

When constructing a new building, the cost of making it accessible is negligible. Some people have said you could add 1 percent to the cost of the building. This certainly isn't much to make a building accessible if you're starting with a new building. But I've also heard it said that it doesn't cost much to comply in an existing building. We've done a lot of work over the last few years for private and governmental entities that are trying to comply, and going into full compliance is very expensive in many cases. In most cases, it's very expensive to go back and retrofit an existing building. That doesn't mean that you cannot become accessible and work something out that doesn't cost a lot of money, but generally it is fairly expensive to comply.

I heard some people in the audience express concern that they understood what the needs were, but their management or their county commissioner wasn't particularly inclined to spend the money for ADA improvements. What I'm going to go through is a process that has helped keep our clients out of court and that has brought them into compliance with the law. After you go through the process with clients, they begin to understand what the intent of the law is and why it makes good business sense to be in compliance with the ADA.

Last year, some of the highest ranking staff in the Department of Justice participated in a three-part satellite broadcast to centers all over the country where people could phone in questions. The standard answer from Justice Department staff was, "We will get back to you."

I have never received a clear answer from the Department of Justice. It has made me, as an architectural professional, very conservative. We do a lot of work with the ADA, and in advising our clients we feel we must go with the most conservative answer. An example would be putting a table beside a checkout counter and having someone work at that table. If we audited that library, we would recommend that the counter be made accessible.

If you haven't already had an audit of your facilities, you will find that the results come back on the conservative side, usually the most expensive solution. There are different ways to comply. An example could be a drinking fountain. If you already have a drinking fountain that is so high that someone cannot access it in a wheelchair, you could put up a paper cup dispenser. For institutional owners, it becomes a management nightmare to deal with all the paper cup dispensers and usually they opt to go ahead and put in a second drinking fountain. But for a small business or a small office building that has on-site management, a paper cup dispenser may be appropriate and cost-effective.

Everyone here has heard about the self-assessment that all governmental entities, all Title II facilities, must have had completed by January 26, 1994. As part of the self-assessment, they had to develop a transition plan. The transition plan, in effect, addresses structural changes. The structural changes by definition under the ADA are any of those physical changes that must be made to a building to make the building accessible.

By law, once you had completed your transition plan, you had until July 26, 1994, to make all those changes if you are a Title II entity. Title III organizations were required to be in compliance as of January 26, 1992. Since then, you have been liable to be sued by anybody who cannot gain access to your facilities. Likewise, if you are a Title II organization, a governmental entity, you can still be sued, even if you are in the process of completing your self-evaluation. (These are the kinds of suits that are being filed in Texas and, I'm sure, elsewhere around the country.)

Conduct an Audit

To prepare yourself, and to find out how you're going to comply, you should have an audit. The survey will be a checklist of what's in your facility: whether the slope of the ramps is too steep; whether there are handrails on those ramps; whether the handrails are the right height, the right diameter, and with enough extension at the top and the bottom of the ramp;

whether the ramp has too long of an incline before it has a resting spot. There are thousands of such details in the ADAAG.

I would recommend two options for conducting an audit. If you have the staff to do it yourself, use the *BOMA International's ADA Compliance Guidebook*, probably the best booklet available. It costs about $30 and it is copyrighted. If you are going to use it, you may need to buy several copies because one booklet only covers one building. If you decide to conduct the audit of your facility yourself, it is probably one of the best documents available.

Another way of conducting an audit is to hire a professional—an architect, an accessibility specialist, someone who is knowledgeable concerning the ADA—to survey your property. When you're interviewing candidates, ask to see how they are conducting their survey, ask to see a sample report. If they don't have a detailed checklist, either ask more questions or talk to somebody else, because there are so many details. The report can come in many forms and will depend upon what kind of an organization you are and what you value.

If you're a large institutional client, if you have many library buildings, or if you're part of a university with many buildings, you probably should have the report prepared in database or spreadsheet format. Information should be submitted on a diskette as a part of the final report to your facilities staff so that the vice president for financial affairs (or the business manager, or the city manager, or whoever is responsible for your budget) can manipulate the data to pull out items and calculate how to work them in to the current or future budget. The report should include the name of the problem, the standard, the deficiency, and a recommendation. You also should have an estimated cost of compliance, because the costs do mount up: It can be very expensive. One of the things that the representative from the Department of Justice said is that there is just about no way that you're going to defend yourself in court by saying that you don't have the money. There is *always* some way that you can find the money.

Priorities

Your consultant can advise you, and can prioritize the work that needs to be done in accordance with the ADA guidelines. There are four priorities established under Title III. (We have included the miscellaneous items from their fourth priority in our third priority.) The first priority is getting somebody on the site, to the front door, and through the door. The people who sponsored and pushed this law through Congress say they want to get into the building. They don't care if the toilet is accessible if they can't get into the building. So the first priority is getting on the site, being able to park, being able to get from a car or a bus into the front door. The second priority is being able to function inside the building. In a library your second priority will be making everything that has to do with being a library functional and accessible. The third priority is restrooms.

In helping determine those priorities, you can take the standard set up under ADAAG, or you could employ a disabilities group to help you. It could be an ad hoc or a standing committee of representatives from the disabled community who could tell you what their priorities are, and you could follow those priorities. The third item is an action plan. Once you've completed the audit and you've established your priorities, develop a work plan outlining what you're going to do, when you're going to do it, and how you're going to do it. Then implement it, and implement it in the way that you said you would.

Employee Accommodation

In dealing with employee accommodation, one cannot overstress that the real barriers are not architectural, they are attitudinal. When it comes to working with people with disabilities the most important thing is, as the real estate maxim, *location, location, location*. In this case it's *attitude, attitude, attitude*. I highly recommend the American Library Association's "People First" videotape. Another videotape that you may not know about is "Meeting People with Disabilities," an eighteen-minute tape made by the Texas Rehabilitation Commission featuring its employees. (It is available free from Terry Foster (512) 483-5000.) This is an excellent source for ideas on how staff should work with people with disabilities when they come into a facility. One of the books I recommend is *Meeting the Needs of People with Disabilities: A Guide for Librarians, Educators, and Other Service Professionals* (Oryx, 1990).

I want to mention a few of the devices that meet the needs of people with disabilities that are visible in the workplace. In the office of a woman at the Texas Blind Commission is a piece of art bought by her husband for her when she was in New Orleans because she couldn't appreciate art the way that sighted people do. It is part of a three-dimensional relief on the wall of her office. Most people can look at art; she can reach up and feel it. Her rolodex and the label on her filing cabinet are in Braille and the files in her drawers are in Braille. She has a device that can punch names and telephone numbers on business cards which she can then file in a box to consult at will. She uses an old Braille typewriter, which has basically been replaced by a computer, and a regular printer and a Braille printer.

In another office is a device called a voice enunciator. An employee types into a computer and whatever she types is enunciated for her. She also has a recording device for the blind, a Kurzweil machine, and a battery-powered device called "Braille and Speak," which she can use to type notes to be downloaded into her computer.

A telecommunications device for the deaf is used by a woman who can speak very well but can't hear. When someone needs to get in touch with her, she may not be looking at her phone, so she carries a vibration beeper at all times. When someone calls her beeper, it vibrates, and she looks to see what the number is and calls back through her TDD. Just to the left of her computer terminal screen is a mirror so she can see people standing at the entrance to her office cubicle. (How much does a mirror cost at K-Mart?)

Questions from the Audience

I was wondering how the ADA affects temporary buildings that are being used between the time that the old building is closed down and the new building is built.

They have to be accessible.

Must they follow the same stringent standards as for a new building?

Officially, yes. Again, if you're trying to comply and you're trying to provide the services, I think that attitude, trying to comply, prevents lawsuits. The rule is that even a temporary building must comply. You may have to find some middle ground there, if you have financial constraints.

Does the fact that they are trailers make a difference?

The only trailers of which I'm aware that don't have to comply are temporary trailers and portable toilets on a construction site used exclusively by construction personnel. If anybody has been to an outdoor festival recently, you have probably seen portable toilets that are designed for wheelchair use.

In terms of the ADA, Title II applies to state and locally funded buildings and Title III applies to private. In what category do federal buildings fall?

The federal government is exempt from the ADA. The federal government subscribes to UFAS standards. For instance, a post office could be built by a private individual or private company and rented back to the federal government. That post office is designed to meet the UFAS standards. ADA does not cover the federal government.

CHAPTER FOUR

Historic Properties and the ADA

Michael Howard

I have been charged with discussing a relatively little-known aspect of the ADA and making it understandable and "user-friendly." We'll talk about instances when the historic significance of buildings collides with compliance with the ADA.

> How do you view the ADA?
> Are you rushing to embrace this legislation,
> or do you feel as though . . .

> > First there was *asbestos,*
> > Then came *radon gas* closely followed by
> > *sick building syndrome* . . .
> > Now the ADA?

I hope you leave this session without having that feeling about something as important as the ADA.

During the last presidential campaign, political satirist Molly Ivins gained considerable recognition. Ms. Ivins lives in, and picks on, the great state of Texas. In her 1991 book, *Molly Ivins Can't Say That, Can She?*, she relates an extraordinary moment in Texas legislative history when the Texas Speaker of the House, Gib

Lewis, came to the rescue of the Indigents' Health Care Plan by casting the tie-breaking vote that allowed this legislation to become law, and placing him in the unusual role of champion for the disabled.

Now you must realize that Ms. Ivins is not a great fan of Gib Lewis, for she has been heard to say that "if Gibber's IQ were to increase by 5 percentage points, we would have to water him twice a day." According to Ms. Ivins, Gibber's great moment, being the champion of the disabled, came on Disability Day for the state of Texas, a day dedicated to honor

> . . . handicapped folks for their efforts to get better access to public buildings. We never give them any money for this, but we honor their efforts to get it. Anyway, the Guv issued a proclamation, both houses just resoluted up a storm, and Gib Lewis read all of it without hardly making any mistakes. We were all so proud. Then he looked up at all the handicapped folks who had wedged their wheelchairs into the gallery and said, "And now, will y'all stand and be recognized."[1]

The purpose of this story is not to pick on Gib Lewis, but to illustrate a point regarding *awareness,* especially *managerial awareness* of a public problem:

Michael R. Howard, AIA, is executive vice president of the Mathes Group, an architectural firm in New Orleans. He specializes in fine arts projects and in alterations to existing structures as a consultant and planner, project manager, and master planner.

1. Molly Ivins, *Molly Ivins Can't Say That, Can She?* (New York: Random, 1991), p. 30.

The ADA is often in direct conflict with

your budget and issues of the most cost-effective expenditure of public and private funds;

your operations and the scheduling and management of public and private facilities;

your physical plant goals and the sequence with which you approach proposed future building modifications and/or renovations;

in the case of historic structures, the fundamental historic nature of your building when compliance with the ADA can force change upon, or destroy, the very elements that make your building historic.

Sir Isaac Newton said, "If I am great, it is because I stood on the shoulders of giants." I will not debate with you here the value of history. I only ask you to accept the following two facts:

History and "the historic character of a property shall be retained and preserved. The removal of historic materials or alteration of features and spaces that characterize a property shall be avoided." This is a direct quote from Standard 2 from the Secretary of the Interior's *Standards for Rehabilitation* (revised 1990).

Compliance with the Americans with Disabilities Act of 1990 is both a legal and a moral obligation. Title II of the ADA, which covers state and local government property, states that state and local governments must make their programs and services readily accessible by January 26, 1995.

Title III, which covers commercial structures and places of public accommodations (such as libraries), requires owners to improve accessibility, although work can be deferred until major alterations to a structure are undertaken. In the interim, Title III requires owners to remove physical barriers as time and money permit.

Fundamental Law

History v. the ADA

There is conflict involved if history and the preservation of historic parts of a building appear to collide with the ADA. First of all, you should either be com-

forted or terrified by the fact that there is legal recognition of this problem in the Act. Both Titles II and III recognize that full compliance with the ADA may, in some cases, "threaten or destroy" the historic significance of some buildings. It is for this reason that a methodology has been offered which leads toward a resolution of this potential conflict.

Before we discuss the methodology, we need to answer the question, "When is a building *historic?* Historic buildings covered by the ADA's special provisions are those listed in, or eligible for, listing in the National Register of Historic Places, including contributing buildings in historic districts as well as those designated under state and local laws.

Also, before we discuss the precise methodology for rectifying the conflict, you need to know that "the owner of a historic building must *prove* to the State Historic Preservation Officer (SHPO) or a designee, that the proposed alterations under the ADA would threaten to destroy the features that convey the property's significance." Again, before we discuss the precise methodology, we need to discuss what is considered proof, since without it, you will never reach the methodology stage in the first place.

Most designated historic buildings have nomination forms which are kept on file in the office of the State Historic Preservation Officer. The forms usually include a statement of significance and an architectural description of the property. The owner of a historic building can obtain a copy of the nomination form and glean a list of historic building features from the statement of significance or the architectural description. Such a list might include:

portico entry over main entrance door,

mansard roof, or

decorative interior door moldings.

Next, the owner of a historic building must prepare a list of ADA compliance requirements. Such a list might include:

adding 1:12 ramp at main building entry;

widening interior doorways to comply with ADA-specified width (32 inches).

After completing a list of historic building features and a list of ADA compliance requirements, the owner of a historic building must compare the two lists and identify the conflicts (i.e., a doorway width cannot be increased to ADA standards without destroying the historic detailing of the door's frame, etc.).

Now that we've covered the basics regarding what is historic, why it is historic, what is needed for ADA compliance, and where the conflicts are, we can discuss the precise methodology for resolving these problems.

The Department of Justice has established a consultation process in which the owner of a historic building meets with the SHPO to discuss the conflicts between the maintenance of historic building features and ADA compliance. If the SHPO concurs with the owner that the building's historic features would be threatened or destroyed by ADA compliance, then the compliance requirements can be downgraded to "the minimum requirements for historic preservation." Sounds pretty good, doesn't it? Before we discuss the actual minimum requirements, let's discuss the four perceived basic levels of ADA compliance.

Four Levels of Compliance

Level 1: New Construction

This is, obviously, the most stringent level for ADA compliance.

Level 2: Alteration

ADA compliance for alterations is less stringent than compliance for new construction. The building owner must comply "to the maximum extent feasible." This wording applies to the occasional case where the nature of an existing facility makes it virtually impossible to comply fully with applicable accessibility standards and, in this case, the alteration shall provide the maximum physical accessibility feasible. Under this ruling, the owner must do the best he or she can to comply with the standards and have an eye toward this compliance being tested through litigation. Furthermore, the words "technically infeasible" come into play. Technically infeasible means that the modification has little likelihood of being accomplished owing to existing structural conditions, or other existing or physical site constraints prohibit modification or addition of elements, spaces, or features which are in full and strict compliance with the minimum requirements for new construction.

Level 3: Historic Alterations

Naturally, these requirements referred to as "minimum requirements" or "alternative requirements" are even less stringent than for new construction or alterations.

Level 4: Alternative Methods

Even if the minimum or alternative requirements damage or destroy the historic features which convey a property's significance, a building owner may resort to alternative methods to make the offered programs and services accessible to people with disabilities. Examples include using audiovisual materials and devices to show inaccessible parts of a historic property; assigning persons to assist and guide individuals with disabilities into, or through, inaccessible parts of historic property; adopting other innovative methods.

It should be noted that before an owner complies with alternative methods, he or she has to do his homework with regard to "proof." The historic nature of the building must be proved. Formal compliance with the ADA must be analyzed. Conflicts must be clearly defined and agreed upon by the SHPO. Finally, acceptable alternative methods must be agreed upon by the owner, the SHPO, and in "consultation with interested persons." Interested persons who should be invited to participate in the consultation process include state or local accessibility officials, individuals with disabilities, and organizations representing individuals with disabilities.

Minimum Requirements for Historic Preservation

Obviously, the most common approach for the compliance of historic buildings with the ADA is by complying with the minimum requirements for historic preservation. The minimum requirements are:

An accessible route is required from only one site access point, such as a parking lot, to an acceptable entrance. This is considerably less than the standard 50 percent building access requirements.

The accessible entrance does not need to be the principal public entrance (however, it cannot be locked during normal business hours, and appropriate signage directing disabled persons to that entrance must be provided).

A ramp may be steeper than normally permitted, but the slope may not exceed one-inch rise to six-inch run for a maximum run of two feet, even. This is considerably steeper than the one-inch requirement.

Only accessible unisex restrooms need be provided. This is a greatly relaxed requirement over the ADA standards.

Accessible routes are only required on the level of the accessible entrance, and access is only required to other levels where it is practical. Every level in a historic building may not be required to be accessible if the installation of elevators or lifts proves to threaten or destroy the historic features of the building.

All displays and exhibits must be located where they can be seen by a seated person (44-inch viewing height).

Summary

By now most persons are more comfortable with the ADA and its established process for allowing people with disabilities to enjoy our architectural heritage. Clear and careful thought obviously has been given to this process but that is not to say that the process is perfect or without fault. The process is only as strong and consistent as the individuals who administer it.

A recent building project by my office involved the demolition of an old residence to make way for new construction for a client. The existing residence is, in fact, a 1930s builder's tract house and possesses absolutely no historical significance. However, because the proposed demolition and new construction involved funding and because the building site is located within the Uptown historic district, we were forced to coordinate our work with the SHPO and to follow the "106 process." The 106 process is a review process which

must be completed before the demolition of any historic or potentially historic structure within a historic district involving the use of federal funds.

The SHPO classified the residence as contributing to the overall historic nature of the district and, therefore, recommended against its demolition. Being forced to comply with the requirements of the SHPO and the 106 process, our firm redesigned the entire project, incorporating the "historic residence" into the new construction plans. The new plans required making the historic residence comply with the minimum requirements of the ADA. Naturally, we could not comply with even the minimum requirements without drastic alterations to the building. We appealed to the SHPO to allow us to resort to alternative methods so that we could maintain the "historic nature of the residence."

You guessed it. The SHPO denied all relief from the minimum requirements, stating that the historic elements of the building which he, the SHPO, fought so hard to preserve were not significant enough to warrant relief from ADA compliance. Thus ends the lesson.

On a more positive note, the value of historic structures is recognized. People who are disabled don't want to visit a historic building that has been seriously compromised to make it as totally accessible as new construction; they want to experience the historic environment.

Rather than viewing these requirements as a legislative nightmare, we must look at them positively, and ask, How can we meet this challenge?

Conclusion

The flowchart shown in figure 4.1 best answers the question of how the ADA can coexist with historic architecture.

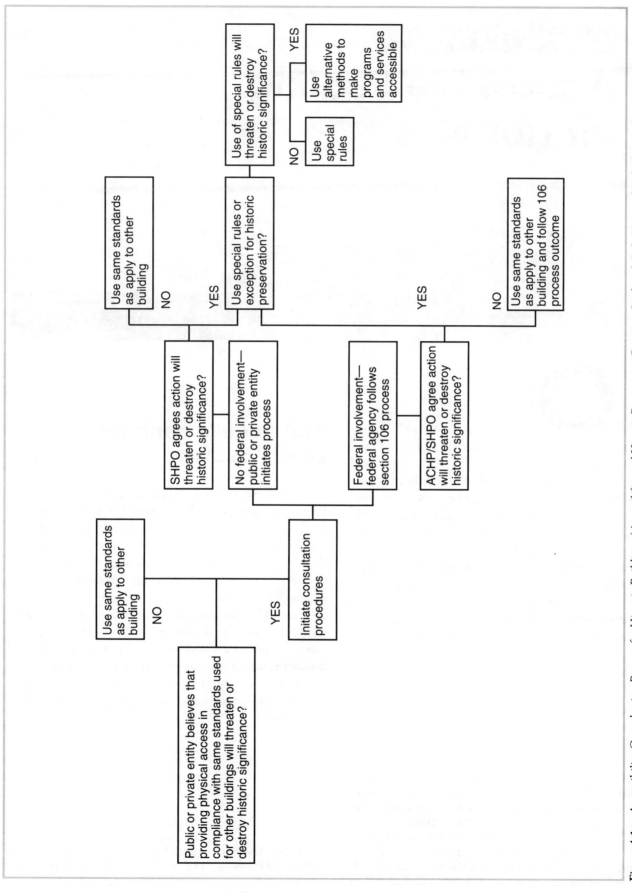

Figure 4.1. Accessibility Consultation Process for Historic Buildings (*Accessibility and Historic Preservation Resource Guide*, ed. Judy Hayward and Thomas Jester, Historic Windsor, 1992). Reprinted with permission.

CHAPTER FIVE
Accessible Seating for Libraries

Elizabeth C. Habich

One of the most basic and ubiquitous services libraries provide users is a place to read and study. If we are to make our library buildings and services accessible to individuals with disabilities, it is critical that this most basic service be made accessible.

This chapter addresses the provision of accessible library seating for people with disabilities and the ADA in three parts: first, a review of the ADA's requirements for library seating (a layperson's interpretation of key provisions); second, a description of what we did in the design of our pre-ADA library building at Northeastern University; and a brief discussion of what we would be required to do differently today.

ADA Requirements for Library Seating

The *ADA Accessibility Guidelines* include several sections detailing general requirements for all types of facilities. Subsequent sections detail additional requirements for specific types of facilities.[1] Section 8 details the additional requirements for libraries, and Section 8.2 addresses reading and study areas.[2] It requires that "five percent or a minimum of one of each element of fixed seating, tables, or study carrels comply with" the sections dealing with space allowance and reach ranges (4.2), and fixed or built-in seating and tables (4.32). It further requires that "clearance between fixed accessible tables and between study carrels shall comply with" the section dealing with accessible routes (4.3).

Elizabeth C. Habich is administrative services officer at Northeastern University Libraries. She served as building projects officer for the planning and construction of their 240,000-square-foot Snell Library, completed in 1990. A frequent speaker on building design issues, Habich provides consulting assistance to libraries planning new and renovated facilities. She earned her M.S. in library and information science from Simmons College and an M.B.A. from Northeastern University.

1. The *Americans with Disabilities Act Accessibility Guidelines* are printed in the *Federal Register* (26 July 1991), vol. 56, no. 144, pp. 35455–35691.

2. Ibid., p. 35668.

Numbers and Distribution of Accessible Seats

In thinking about what this means in terms of actual numbers of accessible seats, consider the following chart:

Total Seats	5%
100	5
500	25
1,000	50
2,000	100

Beyond the absolute number of seats, Section 8.1 of the ADAAG requires that all public areas of the library comply, specifically including "reading and study areas . . . reference rooms, reserve rooms, and special facilities or collections," and you must therefore make accessible areas such as microcomputer labs, AV facilities, group (and individual) study rooms, current periodicals rooms, and archives.

Clear Space

In selecting or designing library seating that meets ADA requirements, ADAAG Section 4.32, Fixed or Built-in Seating and Tables, is most important to consider.[3] It states that:

> If seating spaces for people in wheelchairs are provided at fixed tables or counters, clear floor space complying with 4.2.4 shall be provided. Such clear floor space shall not overlap knee space by more than 19 inches.[4]

The lower diagrams in figure 5.1 illustrate this by showing a 30- by 48-inch clear space partly under the illustrated work surface.

This means that if you are providing seating at an accessible table or carrel, and the carrel is, for example, 24 inches deep, only 19 inches of that depth count toward the 48 inches of clear space you need to allow, and an additional 29 inches of contiguous clear space must be provided.

Clearance

Under-table or under-carrel clearance is also critical because this space must not only accommodate human knees, but also wheelchair arms. Section 4.32.3 requires that at accessible table or carrel seating, knee

---

3. Ibid., p. 35662.

4. That is, measuring 30″ × 48″.

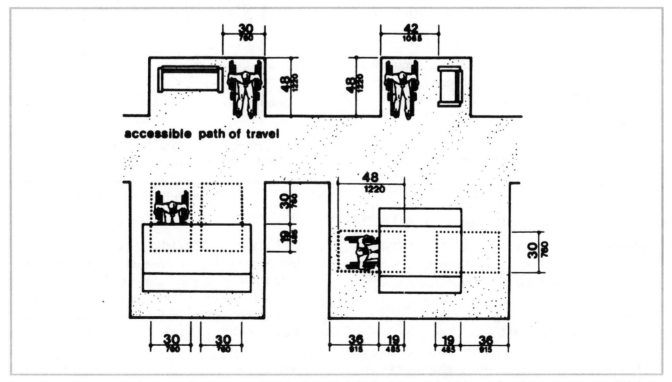

Figure 5.1.   Minimum Clearances for Seating and Tables (ADAAG, *Federal Register* [26 July 1991], vol. 56, no. 144, p. 35663).

spaces shall be at least 27 inches high, 30 inches wide, and 19 inches deep.

This addresses the clear space under the carrel or table's work surface. In evaluating tables, particularly, you must watch out for structural or decorative aprons that may descend beneath the table top. Also watch out for wire management trays, conduits, and other attachments which may protrude from the inside walls of carrels, both those built into newly purchased carrels and those you may wish to add later.

Height

The height of tables and other work surfaces is also important, and Section 4.32.4 requires that "the tops of accessible tables and counters shall be from 28 inches to 34 inches above the finished floor or ground." This standard must be considered in combination with the preceding knee clearance requirement, but allows some flexibility in accommodating different architectural styles of furnishings.

Locating Accessible Seating

In locating these accessible seats, you must comply with Section 4.2, which deals with space allowances and reach ranges, and Section 4.3, which describes accessible routes.[5]

Section 4.2, Space Allowance and Reach Ranges, defines:

wheelchair passage width as 32 inches minimum at a point, and 36 inches continuously (Section 4.2.1), as illustrated by figure 5.2;

width for wheelchair passing as 60 inches minimum for two wheelchairs to pass (Section 4.2.2), as illustrated by figure 5.3;

wheelchair turn space as minimum 60 inches clear diameter to make a 180-degree turn (Section 4.2.3), as illustrated by figure 5.4; and

clear floor or ground space for wheelchairs at a minimum 30 inches by 48 inches (Section 4.2.4), as illustrated by figure 5.5.

You must think about the relation between accessible routes and accessible seating locations when considering where a clear space for a wheelchair can be placed. Section 4.2.4.2, Relationship of Maneu-

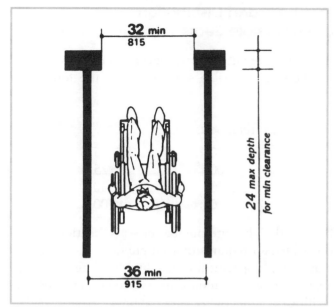

Figure 5.2. Minimum Clear Width for Single Wheelchair (ADAAG, *Federal Register* [26 July 1991], vol. 56, no. 144, p. 35621).

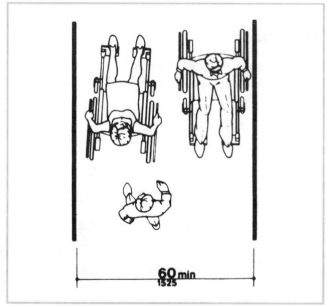

Figure 5.3. Minimum Clear Width for Two Wheelchairs (ADAAG, *Federal Register* [26 July 1991], vol. 56, no. 144, p. 35621).

vering Clearance to Wheelchair Spaces, requires that the clear or ground space must adjoin or overlap an accessible route, or adjoin another wheelchair clear floor space. If the clear floor space is in an alcove, additional maneuvering clearance is required. This requirement could be of particular interest if a library

5. *Federal Register* (26 July 1991), vol. 56, no. 144, pp. 35620–35627.

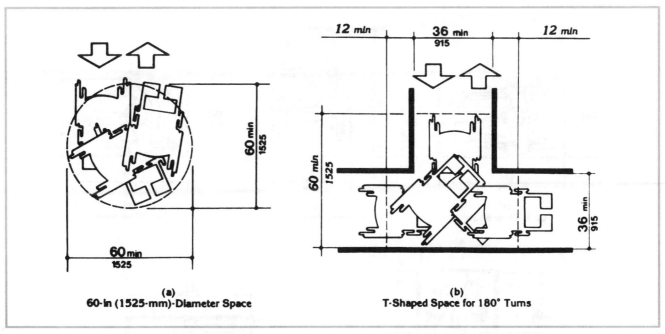

12 min   36 min / 915   12 min

60 min / 1525

36 min / 915

60 min / 1525

60 min / 1525

(a)
60-in (1525-mm)-Diameter Space

(b)
T-Shaped Space for 180° Turns

Figure 5.4. Wheelchair Turning Space (ADAAG, *Federal Register* [26 July 1991], vol. 56, no. 144, p. 35622).

wants to use alcoves for a specialized service (for instance, an OPAC or CD-ROM workstation).

Floor Surfaces

Floor surfaces for wheelchair spaces are also covered by the ADAAG and must comply with Section 4.5, which requires a firm, stable, slip-resistant finish; if the floor is carpeted, it must have a firm or no-cushion backing or pad and maximum pile thickness of ½ inch, with a securely fastened, relatively flush edge (Section 4.5.3).[6]

Access to an Object by Reaching

Where the only access to an object is by *reaching forward*, the maximum height allowed is 48 inches, as required by Section 4.2.5; if the reach is over an obstruction, the maximum height is reduced, according to figure 5.6. It's important to note that worksurfaces themselves constitute an obstruction, as illustrated by figure 5.6, and you may want to think about this when you are positioning an accessible online catalog terminal on an accessible carrel or counter.

Where access to an object is by reaching to the side, as illustrated by figure 5.7, the maximum high reach may be 54 inches and the minimum low reach no less than 9 inches (Section 4.2.6). Again, if the reach is over an obstruction, the permissible reach changes. Acces-

sible routes are described in Section 4.3, which deals with "all walks, halls, corridors, aisles ... and other spaces that are part of an accessible route. ..."

Section 4.3 requirements that most directly bear on planning library seating areas require:

> 4.3.2 (2) At least one accessible route shall connect accessible buildings, facilities, elements, and spaces that are on the same site.
>
> (3) At least one accessible route shall connect accessible building or facility entrances with all accessible spaces and elements ... within the building or facility.

This means, logically enough, you must provide an accessible route to your accessible seating.

Subsequent parts of Section 4.3 set out the characteristics of an accessible route, including:

> 4.3.3 Width: The minimum clear width of an accessible route shall be 36 inches except at doors ...
>
> 4.3.3 Passing Space: If an accessible route has less than 60 inches width, then passing spaces at least 60 inches by 60 inches shall be located at reasonable intervals, not to exceed 200 feet. A T-intersection of two corridors or walks is an acceptable passing place.
>
> 4.3.8 Changes in Levels: ... if an accessible route has changes in level greater than ½ inch, then a curb ramp, ramp, elevator or platform lift ... shall be provided. ...

---

6. Ibid., pp. 35628–35630.

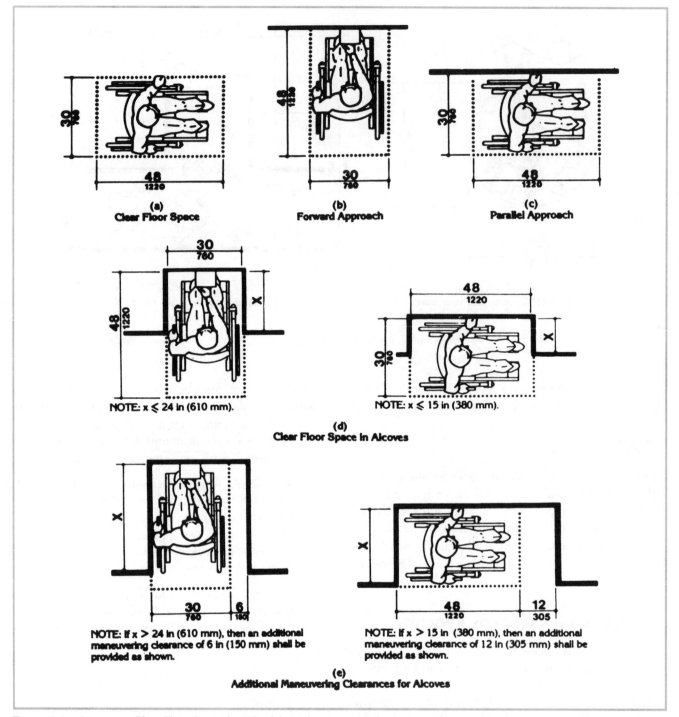

(a)
Clear Floor Space

(b)
Forward Approach

(c)
Parallel Approach

NOTE: x ≤ 24 in (610 mm).

NOTE: x ≤ 15 in (380 mm).

(d)
Clear Floor Space In Alcoves

NOTE: If x > 24 in (610 mm), then an additional maneuvering clearance of 6 in (150 mm) shall be provided as shown.

NOTE: If x > 15 in (380 mm), then an additional maneuvering clearance of 12 in (305 mm) shall be provided as shown.

(e)
Additional Maneuvering Clearances for Alcoves

Figure 5.5.   Minimum Clear Floor Space for Wheelchairs (ADAAG, *Federal Register* [26 July 1991], vol. 56, no. 144, p. 35623).

The first two requirements may affect the layout of your stacks and seating, particularly in areas devoted to collections and study space. The third also covers changes in floor covering, so you must look carefully at transitions from, for example, carpeting to tile floor.

Although the regulations may seem complex, they do make it easier to identify what you need to do to make your library seating accessible.

Planning Accessible Seating in Snell Library

Northeastern University has a significant community of individuals with disabilities and a strong commitment to making the campus accessible. The library shares that commitment. For example, we have one

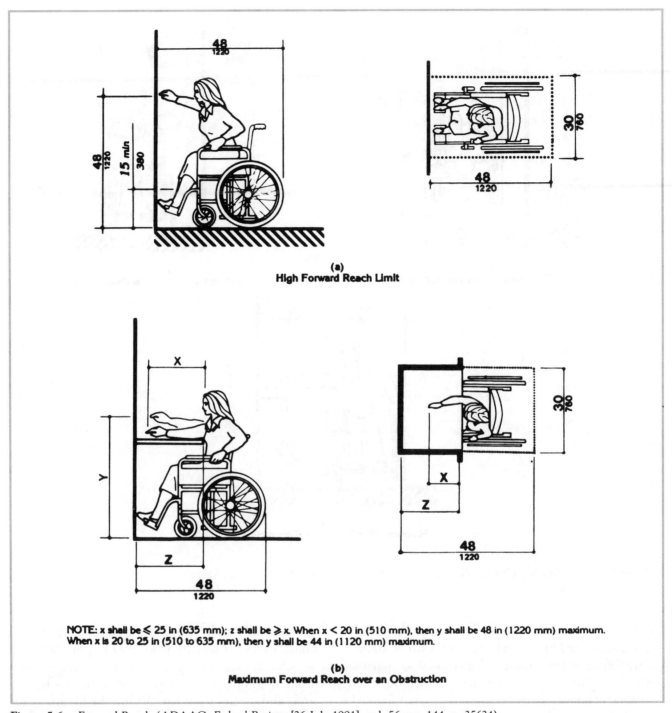

(a)
High Forward Reach Limit

(b)
Maximum Forward Reach over an Obstruction

NOTE: x shall be ≤ 25 in (635 mm); z shall be ≥ x. When x < 20 in (510 mm), then y shall be 48 in (1220 mm) maximum. When x is 20 to 25 in (510 to 635 mm), then y shall be 44 in (1120 mm) maximum.

Figure 5.6.   Forward Reach (ADAAG, *Federal Register* [26 July 1991], vol. 56, no. 144, p. 35624).

TTY/TDD at our reference desk to handle incoming inquiries, and another available for checkout from reserve services for use with the library's on-campus and pay phones. The media center has closed-caption decoders for viewing the video collection and actively collects closed-captioned materials. We have a range of adaptive devices for reading print material and have purchased LP-DOS to use with our CD-ROM workstations, computer labs, online catalog, and staff workstations. Well before enactment of the ADA, we were working proactively to make the library and its programs accessible.

In the mid-1980s, planning began for a new central library for Northeastern's Boston campus, and in summer 1990, Snell Library was opened. The $34-million, 240,000-square-foot facility was designed to provide an excellent environment for study and to be intellectually and physically easy to use. Although our

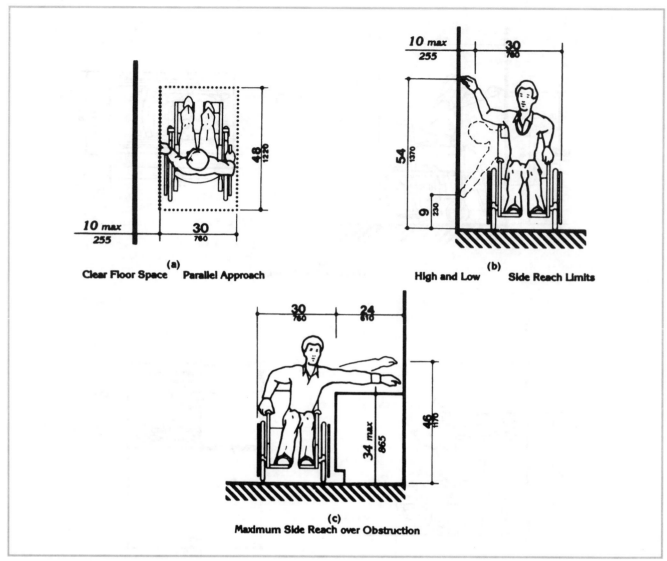

Figure 5.7.   Side Reach (ADAAG, *Federal Register* [26 July 1991], vol. 56, no. 144, p. 35625).

new building was completed before the ADA went into effect, the library worked closely with Northeastern's Office of Handicapped Services (since renamed the Disability Resource Center) to determine the number of handicapped-accessible seats that should be provided, where they should be located, and how they should be designed.

Seating Types and Access Goals

As we planned our new building, we knew we wanted to provide seating accessible to people who used wheelchairs, and we opened a dialogue with the Office of Handicapped Services to identify the clearances required to accommodate wheelchairs, locations easily

maneuvered into by people using wheelchairs, and the number of such seats that we should provide.

Our broad goal was to provide accessible seating in all areas of the library, integrated into each of the study and special-use areas. Within the library we provide approximately 2,800 user seats, including:

almost 2,000 general study and reading seats at carrels, tables, and lounge chairs, of which 455 of the approximately 1,100 carrels are linked to the campus local area network (LAN);

111 microcomputer lab workstations in three distinct labs, including one Macintosh lab, one extended-hours Mac plus DOS lab, and one teaching lab;

89 individual-use audiovisual (AV) access seats, including spaces for RF (radio frequency) distributed video viewing, remote-controlled audio and video listening and viewing, and hands-on AV equipment use;

32 individual studies on two floors;

11 group studies comprising 72 seats, spread over four floors;

72 seats in the library seminar room, and others in the bibliographic instruction room and the group AV room;

56 graduate student study carrels;

45 online catalog access carrels;

16 CD-ROM workstations; and

39 microform carrels.

From this listing, it should be obvious that although Snell Library contains over 2,800 user seats, there are many smaller specialized service areas within it. These presented a major challenge: how to provide a reasonable number of accessible seats for people who used wheelchairs, while maintaining our ability to flexibly meet peak-use demands from both our ambulatory users and people using wheelchairs. We knew we wanted to provide a minimum of one accessible seat in each specialized area, but the total number varied depending on the total number of seats in the area, whether there was further specialized seating within an area, and whether the seating was planned for individual or group use.

For instance, we have one large cluster of about twenty-five online patron access catalog (OPAC) terminals on our main floor, and additional smaller clusters on each upper floor and in the reserve/extended hours area. These were each relatively small areas, but we knew we wanted at least one terminal in each cluster to be handicapped-accessible.

Because some of the media center's seating was planned for both class and individual use, we took a somewhat different approach. Handicapped Services alerted us that class groups might include two individuals who used wheelchairs; so, in areas where we were planning for class use, we provided two accessible carrels per group.

While we felt that the total number of seats available in the general collection and study areas was large enough in relation to anticipated use, and that we could earmark a portion of these for the exclusive use of individuals who use wheelchairs, this was not the case in areas like the media center and the microcomputer labs where we anticipated heavy use in relation to the number of seats.

Fixed-Height and Height-Adjustable Carrels

The solution we developed used a combination of fixed-height and height-adjustable accessible carrels. In the general collection and study areas, we used fixed-height accessible carrels. In specialized areas, with limited total seats, we used either a combination of fixed- and adjustable-height carrels or adjustable-height carrels exclusively.

As part of the interior design process, we wrote functional specifications for all of our carrels and tables. For general use carrels, we specified a 29-inch work surface height, and for carrels housing microcomputer and microform workstations, we specified a 26-inch work surface height. For the handicapped-accessible, fixed-height carrels and tables we specified a minimum 29-inch clearance beneath the work surface, and the work surface height varied somewhat depending on what extended beneath the work surface.

The ADAAG requires a 27-inch clearance beneath work surfaces; the 29-inch clearance we specified was based on Handicapped Services' observation that there was a range of types of wheelchairs in use on our campus and that, although a lower height could accommodate many or most wheelchairs, the 29-inch clearance was needed to accommodate all.

For the adjustable-height accessible carrels, we specified a range of adjustment that would work for both ambulatory and wheelchair-using individuals: between 27 and at least 29 inches' clearance beneath the work surface to accommodate individuals using wheelchairs and, to accommodate ambulatory users, work surface heights of 29 inches for most carrels and 26 inches for carrels housing terminals and microcomputer workstations. (The height adjustments are made with a hand-operated crank which retracts and folds up neatly beneath the carrel worksurface when not in use.)

In considering where the accessible carrels and tables should be placed, we relied again on the expert assistance of Handicapped Services, and placed them where they were visible, on routes which were generally adjacent to a main corridor through stack or seating areas, and where there was room for a wheelchair to be maneuvered into place.

Signage

One mark of our success in integrating accessible seating into the library is that it looks very similar to the seating used by ambulatory users. However, we decided there needed to be a way for individuals who wished to use the accessible seating to easily identify it. So, as part of the library's signage program, we affixed decals with the standard access symbol to each element of accessible seating, where it was visible from the predominant path of user traffic.

Snell Library Seating and the ADA

Most of the work resulting from the discussions between the library and Handicapped Services would still be valid in the era of the ADA. The carrel and table clearances exceed those required by the ADA,

the number of carrels in specialized areas is generally fine, and our accessible seating is located on accessible routes. If we were working on this project today, the total number of seats would need to be increased somewhat to comply with the ADAAG, but the number of seats we do have appears to meet the needs of our user community.

And, although the requirements for providing handicapped-accessible seating are now public law, one thing I would not change is the process of meeting with Handicapped Services and discussing with them the needs of our university's specific community. Among specific instances where their expertise helped us was in making sure carrel and table clearances would accommodate the range of wheelchairs in use on our campus. Their observations carried an immediacy and authority beyond that of written standards, and the process of communication helped build an effective working relationship benefiting the students, faculty, and staff of the Northeastern University community.

CHAPTER SIX
Adaptive Technology

Barbara T. Mates

Even before the passage of the Americans with Disabilities Act, I was often asked, "Why do we need adaptive technology? Isn't there a National Library Service that lends Braille and cassette books?" Rather than pointing out the fact that only 2,000 titles are selected each year for special media, I've used a short review of current history to answer this question:

Current(?) Reference Material and Recent History

1960
First and Last Braille Encyclopedia Published

John Glenn Completes First U. S. Orbit of Earth

Death of John F. Kennedy

Passage of the Civil Rights Act

Deaths of Robert F. Kennedy and Martin Luther King, Jr.

Neil Armstrong Walks on the Moon

Barbara T. Mates is regional librarian for the blind and physically handicapped at the Cleveland Public Library. She was one of the first to install CD-ROMs with multiple format output (Braille, voice, large print) for reference service. She authors the "Adaptive Technology" column for *Computers in Libraries*, and is the author of *Library Technology for Visually and Physically Impaired Patrons* (Meckler, 1991).

1970
Last Large Print Encyclopedia Published

President Nixon Visits China

South Vietnam Surrenders, Ending the Vietnam War

Vietnam Peace Agreement Signed

1980
The *World Book Encyclopedia* Recorded Using a New Indexing Method for Retrieval of Information

AIDS Virus Discovered

Gorbachev Succeeds Chernenko as Premier of Former USSR

Birth of the PC, Providing Potential for Limitless Peripherals and Adaptive Technology

In other words, if we searched through the last Braille encyclopedia produced we would find space travel still a dream; if we searched the last large-print encyclopedia we would not find out about nuclear reactors and Three Mile Island; a search of the last recorded encyclopedia would not have any information on the AIDS virus. Yet, we know that there is a wealth of information published on all of these subjects. With adaptive technology you can offer patrons access to materials as they are published.

Technology, Your Library, and the ADA

Adaptive technology affects almost every part of the library's operation. I worked in a neighborhood branch library at one time, and I realize that all patrons do not want or need reference service or recreational reading. Many people use libraries for information referrals, photocopier use, or as a quiet place to do correspondence. There are also patrons who use the library for entertainment needs by borrowing records or videotapes. And there are patrons who use the library to attend lectures or movies.

I will briefly discuss some very basic and relatively inexpensive items that will make you and your library accessible. I must emphasize that you do not have to purchase all of the suggested items at one time, and that an open and positive staff attitude toward persons with disabilities is more important than any equipment.

You could probably purchase adaptive technological items for under $25,000 that would completely open your library to most persons having disabilities. This package would include

accessible furnishings

a personal computer (PC) equipped with laser printer with large-print font; compact disc (CD) drive and CDs; print-to-Braille translator software; voice translator and output receiver; Braille interface or access for user's own equipment; and alternate keyboards

closed circuit television (CCTV)

optical character recognition (OCR) text scanner

telecommunications devices for the deaf (TDD)

closed-captioned and audio-described videos

tape recorder and tape collection.

One of the most basic and heavily used adaptive devices a library can purchase is a closed circuit display (CCD) or a closed circuit television (CCTV). These devices "take a picture" of the items placed on a platform and play it back on the monitor. The size of the print or picture could be enlarged up to eighty times by adjusting a switch. Although this is a tedious way to read a book, in theory it could be done. It is the ideal solution for reading newspapers, correspondence (including handwritten), and to view photographs and diagrams. It can be very helpful for people with vision impairments who want to maintain their independence by enabling them to read bills and write checks. Some CCTV models can also be interfaced with a personal computer and will enlarge whatever is displayed on the monitor.

The personal computer and the technological adaptations that have been made over the last five years have been called "the equalizer," "my missing parts place," and "my eyes" by people with disabilities. A totally adaptive personal computer is equipped with large-print access, voice output, and Braille output.

Large Print

Large-print access is a good starting point when you begin to adapt your equipment. Large print is defined as print that is 14-point. One of the first and least expensive items to purchase is large-print key tops for typewriters and keyboards. For under $20, you can help the patron who does not know touch-typing to see the keys on the keyboard. Unlike the keys on regular keyboards these peel-and-stick letters fill the entire key space.

At about $200, an economical method for enlarging the typeface on a personal computer (PC) or video display terminal monitor is with a Fresnel lens such as the Compu-Lenz, which slips over the monitor and magnifies the print three times. This is a fixed method of producing large print and the user can not change it. The lens will not fit over all monitors, and you do lose resolution at the edges of the monitor.

There are other, more expensive methods that yield better results. A 21-inch Super VGA monitor will allow the user to read the entire screen without any distortion. The method which allows the most latitude is to attach the computer to a CCTV or to install a software package. Specialized software allows the user to adjust the display and make the letters wider or bolder, or reverse the background. Individuals have different visual disabilities and each are aided in different ways.

Capacity for hard copy output is equally important. All that is needed for good large-print output is a laser printer with a font that yields a clear, bold typeface of at least 14-point.

Voice Output

Voice output on a personal computer is akin to having a reader read aloud what is on the screen. While an unaccustomed ear might think the voice unintelligible, it begins to sound normal after about five minutes of listening. Synthetic voice output, however, is improving.

Voice output requires installation of a speech translator and a voice card. Users turn on the translator with a few keystrokes and proceed to load whatever programs they want to access. There is true skill involved in learning to use the program well. As with any software program, the more you use it, the better you become at it.

Braille Access

The personal computer is also an important avenue into Braille access. It works this way: A unit called refreshable or paperless display is interfaced with the PC. As the cursor moves from letter to letter, solenoid pins raise and lower, forming Braille cells, which allow the users to read the screen with their fingertips. The pins follow the cursor.

To create Braille hard copy you need a print-to-Braille translator and a Braille embosser. The translator is software that will take anything written in ASCII and translate it into Braille. The embosser works like any printer; give the command to print and you get Braille.

Alternate Keyboards

All of the items discussed above are aids that will allow the patron with a visual impairment to read information on the PC. But patrons who are physically unable to reach and type commands on a standard keyboard need another tool. This is where alternate keyboards are appropriate.

There are membrane keyboards that allow for a lighter downward pressure on the keystroke. The area of each key is also larger, allowing users with limited control of their hands (for instance, people with cerebral palsy) to have more latitude in movement. A mini keyboard allows the user without much wrist movement (i.e., arthritis), but good control, to type in commands.

Once your PC is equipped with these adaptations, whatever you purchase for your patrons without disabilities can be used by persons with disabilities. Adaptive CD-ROM access has allowed persons with disabilities to access current information, as does ac-cess to various online databases. Many other types of input/output devices for the PC are also available.

Additional Equipment

Optical character recognition (OCR) reading machines are readily available and have improved considerably since Raymond Kurzweil's original reading machine. They can be portable or attach to a PC and are relatively easy to use, relatively inexpensive, and less finicky than they used to be. Simply described, the machine scans the text and translates it into a format which can be directly read by the user, using the same principles as described for the PC. The equipment does require training to use, is finicky when it comes to fonts, and does not read handwriting. But it would still help readers in need get the gist of most print documents and in some instances allow them to read verbatim all text in a document.

Thus far I have emphasized technology for accessing texts and the printed word, but how would your potential patrons be able to call your library or carry on a conversation with your staff if they were hearing-impaired, or unable to physically speak in a manner in which they could be understood? A device called a text telephone that has two recognized abbreviations, TDD and TTY, can be installed at a service desk. It is a telephone that allows the caller to type questions or comments into the phone instead of speaking and have it read at the receiver's end. All you do to install it is to put the phone jack into the socket. You probably will want to attach it to a signaling device (such as a telephone) to alert staff when the unit is ringing. You should install it where patrons can make short emergency calls. Minimal training is involved with learning how to use a TDD; once trained in TDD etiquette, staff will quickly pick up the abbreviations.

Common Abbreviations Used for TDD Communications

TTY = Teletypewriter (precurser to the TDD)

GA = Go ahead (I'm finished typing, your turn)

SK = Stop key (conversation over, hang up)

CUZ = Because

HD = Hold, please

PLS = Please

OIC = Oh, I see

U   = You

UR   = Your

CD   = Could

Q   = Question mark

R   = Are

NBR = Number

SHD = Should

TMR = Tomorrow

Although the TDD is not marketed as an in-person communication device, it can be used to carry on a conversation simply by allowing each person in turn to type their conversation. The typed conversation appears in the window.

There are other inexpensive pieces of technology that will aid your staff in communicating with the patron who is hearing-impaired. Easy Listener allows the patron in need of voice amplification to hear without having the speaker shout. The user simply slips on the headphones and turns on the amplifier, while the speaker turns on the transmitter and speaks. While this is a good solution for a one-on-one dialogue, it would not work in an audience or group setting. Phonic Ear Easy Listener FM Hearing Assistance System and the National Captioning Institute's Audio-Link devices allow a person to sit anywhere in the audience and hear every word the speaker is saying. While the technical principles are different, the results are the same—persons with hearing impairments can attend programs and not miss any dialogue.

Safety Measures

If your library is large and your alarm system is "dated" (e.g., many facilities only have a sound alarm for emergency evacuations rather than one which also has a strobe that flashes when the alarm is sounding) and you allow patrons to "roam" the stack areas, you might consider purchasing a "silent pager." With this, staff could alert patrons unable to hear the fire alarm. You should have emergency evacuation plans printed and given to patrons when they pick up the pager, which will alert them to look around for signs of smoke or for people moving toward an exit.

Conclusion

I must emphasize again the fact that it is not necessary to purchase all the adaptive equipment at one time. Purchasing audio-described or closed-captioned videos (when available) does not cost any more than purchasing standard videos and all can use them. As with any purchase, find a vendor who will take time to consider where you and your library are in your quest to make it accessible for all—the type of equipment you have and want to use, and what you want to accomplish in a set time period. Involve your patrons with disabilities in the planning process—they more often than not know what is the latest or greatest and what to save your money on. Finally, even if you cannot purchase anything, attitude will go a long way. If we don't have a positive attitude, people with disabilities won't get far.

Vendors of Adaptive Technology Products

The following list of vendors of adaptive technology products is by no means complete. It was compiled to give you a start in your search for equipment and not meant to be an endorsement by LAMA or the American Library Association. Additional vendors can be found in periodicals such as *Closing the Gap*, which reviews adaptive products and publishes an annual resource directory, and Trace Center's Co-Net CD, which gives basic information on products and includes pre-addressed, pre-written letters to producers. All you add is your name and address requesting information on their products.

Key to Products Available

V = blind or visually impaired
D = deaf- or hearing-impaired
P = physically impaired
L = learning disabled, needing voice output

A I Squared   V
P.O. Box 669
Manchester Center, VT 05255
802-362-3612

American Captioning Institute D
5203 Leesburg Pike
Falls Church, VA 22041
703-998-2400

American Communication Corp. D
1040 Roberts St.
East Hartford, CT 06108
203-289-3491

American Printing House V
  for the Blind
P.O. Box 6085
Dept. 0086
Louisville, KY 40206
502-895-2405

American Thermaform V, L
2311 Travers Ave.
City of Commerce, CA 90040
213-723-9021

Arkenstone, Inc. V, L
1185 Bordeux Drive, Suite D
Sunnyvale, CA 94089
408-752-2200 or 800-444-4443

Arts Computer Products V
33 Richdale Ave.
P.O. Box 604
Cambridge, MA 03140
800-343-0095 or 408-752-2200

AT&T Special Needs Center D
2001 U.S. Route 46
Suite 310
Parsippany, NJ 07054
800-233-1221

Berkeley Systems, Inc. V, L
2095 Rose St.
Berkeley, CA 94709
510-540-5535

Blazie Engineering V
105 E. Jarretsville Rd.
Forest Hill, MD 21050
410-893-9333

BOSSERT Specialties V, P
P.O. Box 15441
Phoenix, AZ 85060
800-776-5885

CEELEX V, L
2535 Seminole
Detroit, MI 48214
313-925-9368

CLEO P
3957 Mayfield Rd.
Cleveland Heights, OH 44121
216-382-9700

Closing the Gap V, D, P, L
P.O. Box 68
Henderson, MN 56044
612-248-3294

ComputAbility Corp. P
40000 Grand River Rd., Suite 109
Novi, MI 48050
313-477-6720

COVOX, Inc. V, L
675 Conger St.
Eugene, OR 97402
503-342-1271

DEMCO V, D, P, L
P.O. Box 7488
Madison, WI 53707-7488
800-356-1200

Descriptive Video Service V
WGBH
125 Western Ave.
Boston, MA 02134
800-736-3099

Designing Aids for P
  Disabled Adults (DADA)
249 Concord Ave., #2
Toronto, ON, Canada M6H 2P4
416-530-0038

Don Johnston P
1000 N. Rand Rd.
P.O. Box 639
Wauconda, IL 60084
800-999-4660 or 708-526-2652

Duxbury Systems V
435 King St.
P.O. Box 1504
Littleton, MA 01460
508-486-9766

Echo Speech Corp. V, L
6460 Via Real
Carpinterea, CA 93013
805-684-4593

Enabling Technology V
3102 S.E. Jay St.
Stuart, FL 34997
407-283-4817

Gallaudet University D 800 Florida Ave., NE Washington, DC 20002 800-672-6720	**NanoPac** P 4833 South Sheridan Rd. Tulsa, OK 74145 918-665-0329
Harris Communications D Dept. GASK 9006 Minneapolis, MN 55408 800-825-6758 or 800-825-9187 (TDD)	**Optelec** V 4 Lyberty Way Westford, MA 01886 800-828-1056 or 508-393-0707
Henter-Joyce V, L 10901-C Roosevelt Blvd. St. Petersburg, FL 33716 800-336-5658	**Phone TTY** D 202 Lexington Ave. Hackensack, NJ 07601 201-489-7889 or 201-489-7890 (TDD)
Highsmith Co., Inc. V, D, L, P W 5527 Highway 106 P.O. Box 800 Fort Atkinson, WI 53538-0800 800-558-2110	**Phonic Ear** D 3880 Cypress Dr. Petaluma, CA 94554 800-227-0735 or 707-769-1110
Hoolean, Corp. V P.O. Box 230 Cornville, AZ 86325 602-634-7517	**Potomac Technology** D 1010 Rockville Pike, Suite 401 Rockville, MD 20852 301-762-4005 or 301-762-0851 (TDD)
HumanWare V, L 5245 King Rd. Loomis, CA 95650 800-722-3393 or 916-652-7253	**Prentke-Romich** P 1022 Heyl Rd. Wooster, OH 44691 800-642-8255
ILA (Independent Living Aids) V, L 27 East Mall Plainview, NY 11803 800-537-2118	**Raised Dot Computing** V 408 S. Baldwin St. Madison, WI 53703 800-257-9595 or 608-257-9595
Innoventions V 5921 S. Middleton Rd., #102 Littleton, CO 80123-2877 800-524-6554	**Seeing Technologies** V 7074 Brooklyn Blvd. Minneapolis, MN 55429 612-560-8080
L S & S V, D, L P.O. Box 673 Northbrook, IL 60065 800-468-4789 or 708-498-9777	**Street Electronics** V, L 6420 Via Real Carpinteria, CA 93013 805-684-4593
Maxi Aids V, D, L P.O. Box 209 Farmingdale, NY 11735 800-522-6294	**Telecommunications for the Deaf, Inc.** D 814 Thayer Ave. Silver Spring, MD 20910 301-589-3786 or 301-589-3006 (TDD)
MicroSystems D, P 600 Worcester Rd. Suite B2 Framingham, MA 01701 508-626-8511	**TeleSensory Products (TSI)** V, L 455 N. Bernardo Ave. P.O. Box 7455 Mountain View, CA 94039 800-969-9064

Trace RND Center	V, D, L, P
S-151 Waisman Center	
1500 Highland Ave.	
Madison, WI 53705	
608-262-6966	

UltraTec	D
6442 Normandy Lane	
Madison, WI 53719	
608-273-0707	

University Copy Services, Inc.	P
2054 Bond St.	
University Park, IL 60466	
800-762-2736	

VIS-AIDS	V, L
102-09 Jamaica Ave.	
Richmond Hills, NY 11418	
800-346-9579 or 718-847-4734	

Votrax Consumer Products	V, P
38455 Hills Tech Dr.	
Farmington Hills, MI 48331	
313-442-0900	

Western Center for Microcomputers	V, L
& Special Education	
1259 El Camino Real, Suite 275	
Menlo Park, CA 94025	
415-326-6997	

WesTest Engineering Corp.	P
1470 N. Main St.	
Bountiful, UT 84010	
801-289-7100	

Xerox-Kurzweil Imaging Systems	V, L
185 Albany St.	
Cambridge, MA 02139	
800-343-0311 or 508-977-2000	

People, Assistive Devices, ADAptive Furnishings, and Their Environment in Your Library

Andrea Michaels and David Michaels

Adaptive is a particularly good word because it begins with ADA. We now spend much of our practice addressing issues concerning ADA, not only for new and former clients, but also in educating our clients on the impact ADA will have on their current and future plans in terms of space—cubic area—and the environment which will accommodate and enhance the library's ADA response. We have three goals:

1. To review the nature of disabilities about which we should all be concerned;

2. To assist you in programming, budgeting, and implementing the desired changes; and

3. To illustrate some of the concepts presented.

Libraries serve the broadest constituency, including people with disabilities covered and not covered by

Andrea Michaels and David Michaels, principals, Michaels Associates Design Consultants, Inc., have worked in library planning and interior design for eighteen years. As consultants in the Washington, D.C. area, they have participated in programming, space planning, interior and graphic design, records management, and publication design and production. Both have published articles on library design and planning.

ADAAG. A person with a disability is defined as a person who has, is regarded as having, or has a record of having a permanent or temporary physical or mental impairment that substantially limits one or more "major life activities" (caring for oneself, performing manual tasks, walking, seeing, hearing, speaking, breathing, learning, and working). Often, when people discuss the Americans with Disabilities Act, they think of the common adult disabilities.

Focus of Guidelines

One out of five people in the U.S. is disabled. We tend to think of ADA in terms of common disabilities but, in fact, the ADAAG primarily addresses only *some* of the following categories:

Nonambulatory

Two million people in the United States are confined to wheelchairs. We tend to think of wheelchair occupants in a standard chair, pushed or operated by rolling. But there are many sizes and types of wheelchairs. There are sport wheelchairs, which are smaller, narrower, and lower, with fewer places to put things.

The seat heights, arm heights, and styles vary. A 27-inch clear space under a table may be appropriate, or it may not. Electric wheelchairs are heavier, controls are high, and the steering mechanism may interfere with a work surface. Some wheelchairs are available, however, with swing-away arms in conjunction with standard work surfaces.

Semi-ambulatory with Assistive Device

People with canes, walkers, or crutches are sometimes overlooked. We must consider the unskilled disabled or recently disabled who may need more space until familiar with their device.

Blind

We think of blind people as being non-sighted people who read Braille or use a cane. But, according to Judy Dixon at the Library of Congress Library for the Blind and Physically Handicapped, there are only 20,000 people in the United States who actively use Braille. There are 100,000 more blind people who *can* use Braille to some extent. There are also blind people who don't read Braille but who may use a reader. In that case, they will require seating for two, and perhaps a place for a guide dog. (Although water dishes are not required for trained dogs in most climates, in drier regions they are desirable.)

Visually Impaired

There are 8.5 million people who have visual impairments that require glasses or other assistive devices.

Deaf

There are deaf, non-hearing people who sign and don't speak.

Hearing-Impaired

There are hearing-impaired people who sign but do speak; 21.5 million have a hearing disability; and men tend to be more affected by hearing disabilities than women.

Common disabilities, not specifically addressed in ADAAG, may also be a part of your constituency. They include

arthritic (31 million people) and other individuals who have difficulty lifting, reaching, and carrying.

speech limitations, either because of a neuromuscular problem or unfamiliarity with the predominant language in your library or area.

poor balance.

difficulty interpreting information.

limitation of stamina.

difficulty in sitting.

difficulty in using upper extremities.

difficulty in using lower extremities.

disease: contagious or non-contagious.

debilitating conditions: cerebral palsy, epilepsy, muscular dystrophy, multiple sclerosis, cancer, heart disease, diabetes, mental retardation, emotional illness, specific learning disabilities, HIV disease, tuberculosis, drug addiction, alcoholism.

size: vertically challenged or extremely wide.

age-related disabilities. We need to accommodate the young disabled population. Children, for example, are not presently covered by ADAAG. Also, our population is aging. We will soon have more people over 60 than at any time in our history. Some disabilities occur as people get older:

- vision: older workers have more difficulty perceiving colors and contours, usually defined by slight color changes due to shadows and highlights.

- mobility or loss of dexterity (this also affects some children).

- hearing: 30 percent of older Americans experience hearing loss, frequently most noted after age 45.

cultural diversity and changing work styles.

personal space: needs vary with culture, style of work, or learning. Shift work entails additional personal storage and task separation. Interdependent work and shared technologies demand additional space.

noise-tolerance threshold: varies with the person, disability, device, and task; most employees wish to concentrate without noise.

With understanding and recognition, it is possible to change individuals' attitudes and change responses from negative to positive about any of these disabilities. Staff members should be sensitized to various needs and appropriate responses. The ADA doesn't legislate logic. You should anticipate your particular response to assistive devices and the ADA. In thinking about individual disabilities, consider the whole gamut of disabilities. Think about the tasks, about how they can be accommodated, and then think about the cost of compliance when you consider all those factors. The ADA doesn't give very many suggestions for those uncommon disabilities. They give virtually no space guidelines for assistive devices, and many manufacturers don't give any guidelines on optimal use of their equipment.

Assistive Devices

Barbara Mates (*see* chapter 6) reviewed a range of assistive devices that are relatively inexpensive, or at least gradually decreasing in cost. I'd like you to think about the meaning of an assistive device. We think of machines in this context. But other means of assistance are companions—people and service dogs. Although we think of only blind people as requiring leader dogs, service dogs also help the mobility-impaired, and hearing dogs assist individuals with hearing impairments. At rest, service dogs require two to three square feet of floor space with a minimum of 14 inches' clearance overhead.

In cases where the assistive device is equipment, it is important to understand the nature of the device. The following questions must be answered for adequate planning: What do these devices look like? How big are they? What are the wiring needs? How are they used? What is used in conjunction with the device? Is other equipment used in a particular sequence? Where are the controls? Must LED screens (or other signals) be visible? Where is the on/off switch? What is the appropriate environment for the device and for the user? Who is or are the user(s)? Is keyboarding required? What is the visual acuity of the user? What is the duration of use? What is the task? How much light is required? The amount will depend on the task, on the equipment, and on the individual. How many are required? Where will they go?

Universal Workplace

We've heard about the universal workplace. Once everyone has such an accommodating space, what may or should be done to address specific needs? I'd like to urge you to purchase a copy of James Mueller's excellent publication, *The Workplace Workbook 2.0: An Illustrated Guide to Workplace Accommodation and Technology*, and to briefly review the following considerations:

Provide a visual or tactile backup. Use friendly sounds for information and ugly sounds for urgency—in mid-range frequencies.

The subject of lighting in libraries deserves its own preconference. As Mueller recommends, avoid strong back lighting and maintain even, non-glare lighting at one-third of task-lighting level, at not less than 30 degrees to the line of sight. Increase lighting on LCD displays.

Mark emergency equipment conspicuously, and mark accessible evacuation routes with the accessibility symbol.

Position storage at a level of 20 to 52 inches above the floor and as close to the work surface as is practical—providing assistance for higher storage, and avoiding drawers deeper than 12 inches. For those with limited stamina, provide a powered cart or scooter for mobility to and around large storage areas. Note that additional space will be required to use and store the equipment.

Almost eight million workers report difficulty in sitting. In addition to the items noted in chapter 5, install "rising assist" cushions for those with problems. Provide full armrests, full backrests, and stable bases or swivel bases with an adjustable recline feature, and a foot step or stool for shifting weight at standing stations.

Modifications

Workers throughout the United States experience disabilities that may be affordably and simply accommodated. Although Mueller's book gives many options, I'd like to mention some highlights.

Difficulty in Lifting, Reaching and Carrying

Provide desktop file organizers, mechanical reachers, raised edges and lazy susans. Stabilize keyboards and copy stands or provide articulating arms. When computers and associated assistive devices are included, note how quickly a standard 60-inch by 30-inch desktop fills up.

Difficulty in Using Lower Extremities

Provide a rising assist cushion or chair, powered carts, or scooters; secure supports and work surfaces allowing clearance for wheelchair controls and arms. Provide space to use the devices.

Balance

Over four million workers report poor balance from minor or chronic conditions. Suggestions to assist workers in compensating for poor balance include full backrests and seat belts and cushions added to seating, along with full armrests, backrests, and stable bases; provision of a shoulder bag or pack or cart for carrying materials or a scooter for moving around large areas, with convenient space for storage when not in use.

Difficulty Interpreting Information

The *Workplace Workbook* illustrates accommodative modifications to computers (and other items) for those employees who have difficulty in interpreting information, such as covering unneeded keys, simplifying means for input, scanners, and voice recognition equipment. Note that additional space is required for the equipment. Room must be available for paperwork, opening mail, and sorting.

Limitation of Sight

Sight limitations affect 700,000 U.S. workers as a chronic condition. The figure is higher for those with minor or temporary conditions. To assist those workers, consider the following accommodations. Add a keyboard shelf at an appropriate height, reduce glare and the reflectivity of the screen, increase illumination with task lighting, use an opaque projector to enlarge images or provide magnifiers and bookstands, provide additional above-surface data and telecommunication and duplex electrical outlets, and add a mirror in the workstation corner. Approximately 130,000 U.S. workers are totally blind. Modifications for their workstations might include:

- At computers: shield unneeded keys, provide tactile or Braille output, or provide optical character recognition with voice output to read documents;
- At the workspace: provide audible indicators for multiple phone lines, calculators and clocks with voice output, cassette recorders for notes or dictation, telephone auto-dialer with tactile markings, shelves instead of binder bins for easier access to materials, and space for a Seeing Eye dog.

Limitation of Hearing

Difficulty in understanding usable speech, either in the presence or absence of amplification, affects many workers. Modifications include many amplified devices, captioned audiovisual materials, clearly written instructions, TDDs, vibrating pagers, fax, and tunable masking sound. Sound-absorbent surfaces on the exterior walls of offices for hearing-impaired workers and voice muffling devices to reduce distractions from and to coworkers may also help. At workstations, printers have greater importance for the hard-of-hearing. Total deafness also affects nearly as many workers as total blindness. Space implications are not as extensive as are those for sight-assistive devices, but provision of a TDD with a printer, a mirror, less-absorbent walls for enclosed offices, and face-to-face seating arrangements for guests are possibilities that may affect the size and configuration of workstations.

Speech limitations suggest modifications that are included for other impairments. Isolating printer noise, provision of a communication board (or a portable communication device with voice output), and an LCD display or printer are examples.

Purchasing Equipment

When purchasing adaptive devices examine the hardware and discuss use and cost. Remember that assistive devices may be used for both staff and patrons, but that your budget may allow for only one device. It is important to consider all the ramifications of size, function, use, and environment when planning proper accommodation.

Survey your community to ascertain its needs. Conduct an audit of your building and determine how you may not only comply with the Accessibility Guidelines, but also assist users in your community generally as you address the larger issues.

Universal Design

Following is a review of a few points, which cannot be overstressed.

In chapter 5, dimensions of 30 inches wide × 19 inches deep × 27 inches high were mentioned for knee-well clearance. That will allow almost all non-motorized wheelchairs to fit under the surface. If your clientele and budget permit, we recommend adjustable work surfaces with motorized mechanisms.

ADA assumes a wheelchair takes up a space 48 inches long × 30 inches wide. In fact, as previously mentioned, wheelchairs vary widely in size. In a recent survey of everyday chairs, the chairs ranged from 15 to 30 inches wide and from 32 to 47.5 inches long and from 23 to 40 inches high.

More importantly, insofar as adaptive furnishings are concerned, the seat heights varied from 13 to 23.75 inches in height. The back angles varied from 15 to minus 7 degrees. The type of chair an individual has may make a significant difference in how he is able to use the available technology and materials.

Centered drawers and bulky cantilever supports are knee-well obstacles that have no place in twenty-first–century offices. Keep in mind, however, that a keyboard drawer or articulating keyboard arm also restricts the space available in the knee space. If someone has little sensitivity in the lower extremities, injuries sustained by bumping into obstacles may pass unnoticed and may not be treated properly.

In reach ranges, use is the primary consideration. If a tackable panel is used to display documents, then 25 inches are the maximum universal depth for the work surface. If the rear portion will handle storage, then a depth of 30 to 36 inches is appropriate. If overhead storage binders are specified, the work surface depth should not exceed 30 inches, to allow reaching from a seated position.

Add lazy susans to organize tools or reference materials in deep corners.

If a task is document-oriented, provide tiltable surfaces as an overlay or as the entire unit. Individuals using a head or mouth stick or their feet may tip the keyboard to an appropriate angle.

Tables placed in common areas should be of various fixed heights or adjustable—usually from 28 to 34 inches. Female users are far less easily accommodated than their male coworkers. The optimal arrangement for female users is a 25-inch keyboard support which accommodates nearly 54 percent of users, with an optional adjustment range of plus or minus 2 inches to accommodate the remainder of the female population. Twenty percent of the female population required a 23-inch-high keyboard support, whereas 90 percent of the male population required a surface 27 to 28 inches in height. Usually keyboards should be located so that wrist and lower arm are parallel to the floor, but depending on the length of the forearm, it may be higher or lower. The Kinesis keyboard is designed to eliminate the common strains associated with carpal tunnel syndrome.

To relieve or prevent back pain, research indicates spending a portion of the day standing at work surfaces 33 to 45 inches high for manual work and 33 to 48 inches high for terminal work.

For people with difficulty reaching for or grasping, tools should be tethered to the work surface. A ledge at the back and sides can prevent work or tools from sliding off.

Place electric receptacles at the work surface level when possible, but provide a large enough and simple-to-access wire trough. Small and hidden wire management devices are often inadequate, and beyond move-in day, are abandoned.

Criteria for Adaptive Furnishings

Bear in mind that the furniture industry is just getting started providing such products. Steelcase, Haworth, Worden, and Gaylord are companies that have taken leadership roles in research and development and in offering good product systems. You'll want to obtain their reports. The most important criteria are:

> simplicity and reliability;
>
> affordability;
>
> flexibility; and
>
> appearance—compatibility of structure and finishes with other equipment.

Consider how each device should be used within the library. What modifications to the environment are necessary? Where should each be located? Criteria might include

> convenience to an entrance, or perhaps near the elevator on each level, if more than one device of a certain type is available;
>
> proximity to a staffed service desk so staff may assist, if needed, but not so close that normal conversation would be disturbing;
>
> flexibility of space to facilitate growth and change. Plan the area in sufficient detail to permit extra space for personal space, coats, canes, storage for supplies, and equipment, which is not in use at all times.

When we focus on designing for assistive devices, it is also important to remember we're designing for individuals within an overall design concept. It is essential to pay great attention to edges and surface materials which should be durable, aesthetically pleasing and interesting, safe, pleasant to touch, easy to clean, and of sufficient contrast to indicate level changes, overall size, etc.

Conclusion

Nearly the entire scope of the ADA has an impact upon issues of space-use planning. When designing libraries, plan them on a large enough scale, for what is known and also for future growth. Flexibility, always a touchstone for good library design, is more important than ever. The infinite permutations of individuals, their disabilities, and the ever-evolving list of adaptive devices demand elastic environments which can change and grow.

Resource Guide

Periodicals

Closing the Gap
P.O. Box 68
Henderson, MN 56044
612-248-3294
    Bimonthly publication on applications of microcomputer technology for persons with disabilities.

"11th Annual Survey of Lightweight Wheelchairs." *Sports 'N Spokes* 18 (March/April 1993).
    Critical dimensions and specifications for a variety of wheelchairs.

Roatch, Mary A. "High Tech and Library Access for People with Disabilities." *Public Libraries* (March/April 1992): 88.
    Discussion and photographs of technologies for accessing print information by people with disabilities. Good for gauging relative sizes of equipment and need for better, adjustable work surfaces.

Solomon, Nancy R. "Equal Opportunity Design." *Architecture* (December 1991): 101.
    ADA, barrier-free design, accessibility; options, case studies, space planning.

"Specifying Doors and Door Hardware." *Building Operating Management* (Supplement, February 1991).
    Industry trends, ADA, security, education, new technology.

Thompson, Richard. "Equal Access." *Successful Meetings* (May 1991): 42.
    ADA; accessibility guidelines, meetings industry, hotels; compliance guidelines, checklist, consultants.

Books

Mates, Barbara T. *Library Technology for Visually and Physically Impaired Patrons*. Westport, Conn.: Meckler, 1991.
Assistive devices for an adaptive library environment.

Mueller, James. *The Workplace Workbook 2.0: An Illustrated Guide to Workplace Accommodation and Technology*. Washington, D.C.: Dole Foundation, 1992.
Accessibility; ADA; accommodation guidelines; assistive technology descriptions; glossary; resource directory.

Panero, Julius and Martin Zelnik. *Human Dimension and Interior Space*. London: Architectural Press, 1979.
Space guidelines based on human body at various ages.

Brochures

Allie, Paul. *Designing Workstations That Offer Accessibility to Individuals with Disabilities*.
Work surface, storage, workstation, seating, acoustic, and lighting recommendations for special needs.

Arndt, Robert. *Ergonomics and Office Design*. Alexandria, Va.: National Office Products Assn., 1991.
Ergonomics explained for people and the technological work environment.

"Ergonomics in the Healthy Office." *Healthy Office*. Grand Rapids, Mich.: Steelcase, 1992.
Changes in the workplace require special response to maintain good health.

Moss, Charles A. Jr. and Miriam M. Pace. *Planning Barrier Free Libraries: A Guide for Renovation and Construction of Libraries Serving Blind and Physically Handicapped Readers*. Washington, D.C.: National Library Service for the Blind and Physically Handicapped, Library of Congress, 1981.
General guidelines for planning an accessible library, although space considerations are now outdated.

Adaptive Furnishings

DEMCO
P.O. Box 7488
Madison, WI 53707-7488
800-356-1200
1993 ADA update—Products to help you comply with the Americans with Disabilities Act.

Gaylord Bros.
P.O. Box 4901
Syracuse, NY 13221-4901
800-428-3631
Products for library services to the disabled.

Highsmith Co., Inc.
W 5527 Highway 106
P.O. Box 800
Ft. Atkinson, WI 53538-0800
800-558-2110
Focus: The Americans with Disabilities Act, catalog, spring 1993.

HITEC Group International, Inc.
8205 Cass Ave., Suite 109
Darien, IL 60561
708-963-5588
Assistive technology for the deaf and hearing-impaired, since 1982.

Interactive Learning Systems, Inc.
7480 DeMar Rd.
Cincinnati, OH 45243-3560
800-366-3457
Fax 513-561-1862
Ergonomic furnishings for media and learning environments, adaptive products.

Kinesis Corporation
915 118th Ave. S.E.
Bellevue, WA 98005-3855
206-455-9220
Fax 206-455-9233
Ergonomic keyboard.

K I
1330 Bellevue St.
P.O. Box 8100
Green Bay, WI 54308-8100
414-468-2701
Adjustable furnishings to accommodate effective use of assistive technologies.

North Coast Medical, Inc.
187 Stauffer Blvd.
San Jose, CA 95125-1042
408-283-1950
800-821-9319
WorkMod articulating drawer, arm support, foot rest, CRT monitor extension arm, ergonomic seating, etc.

Remstar International, Inc.
4100 Eisenhower Dr.
Westbrook, ME 04092
800-821-0185
Fax 207-854-1610
Automated storage-and-retrieval system.

Steelcase, Inc.
Grand Rapids, MI 49501
800-227-2960
Adjustable furnishings to accommodate effective use of assistive technologies.

Telesensory
455 North Bernardo Ave.
Mountain View, CA 94039-7455
415-960-0920
Fax 415-969-9064
Large-print, image enlargers, synthetic speech, Braille, and tactile systems to assist the vision-impaired.

Ultratec
450 Science Dr.
Madison, WI 53711
608-238-5400 (voice and TDD)
Assistive devices for hearing-impaired.

VTEK
1625 Olympic Blvd.
Santa Monica, CA 90404
213-452-5966
Assistive devices for visually impaired.

CHAPTER EIGHT

Signage and the ADA

Carolyn Johnson

Signage and the ADA? Discussion of the Americans with Disabilities Act usually focuses on employment and accessibility issues. In fact, a four-page article in the September 1991 issue of *American Libraries*, entitled "What Every Librarian Should Know about the Americans with Disabilities Act," failed to mention signage at all.

Yet, signage is the most visible aspect of the ADA. You can look around and notice who is in compliance with signage, and infer from this which institutions are probably in compliance in their provision of other services and in their treatment of people with disabilities. One might even infer from these symbols which institutions are aware of, and sympathetic toward, people who don't fit into categories of "majority," "average," or "normal."

By now you've probably noticed some signs that are a result of ADA: upright handicapped parking signs in addition to the painted spaces in parking lots;

raised letters and Braille dots on restroom signs in Target stores, Wal-Mart, and other national chains; and the same tactile signs on room numbers in hotels, hospitals, and office buildings. But what about libraries? What have we done to our signage to comply with ADA? Well, what should we have done by now?

I'd like to discuss this subject in three parts: new signs that should be added to libraries; signs that must be changed in order to comply with ADA; and signs that should be removed. Within each part I'll describe what you *must* do to comply with ADA, and what you *can* do to make your library a more accommodating place for people with disabilities, and everyone else.

Adding Signage

New signs that you must add include the International Symbol of Accessibility (ISA) at the entrance to your library, if it is accessible by people with disabilities. If any entrance is not accessible, you must provide directions to an accessible entrance. This symbol is also required at all accessible restrooms and areas of rescue assistance.

Signs designating permanent rooms and spaces, whether they are room numbers or names of rooms, must include tactile lettering (i.e., lettering that is a

Carolyn Johnson worked as a reference librarian at several academic and public libraries before joining Arizona State University in 1990 as an instructional librarian. She is in charge of signage on six campus libraries at ASU and has overseen signage projects including renovations, new libraries, ADA compliance, departmental moves, and room renumbering. Johnson also works as a signage consultant.

minimum of 1/32 of an inch thick), upper case, 5/8 of an inch to 2 inches tall, and grade 2 Braille. Permanent spaces are not defined by the law, but it is generally accepted that these include restrooms, stairs, and elevators in any building. Symbols or pictograms are frequently used for these signs, and for equipment, such as volume control telephones, text telephones, and assistive listening systems. All pictograms must have tactile text and grade 2 Braille below the symbol.

Permanent spaces also include classrooms, offices, meeting rooms, auditoriums, as well as the non-public areas of a library: rooms with electrical and mechanical equipment, custodians' closets, and storage rooms. What do you do about those? The law says that each of these rooms shall have its room number displayed 60 inches from the center of the sign to the floor, on the same side of the door as the handle, and far enough to the side of the door frame that a person reading the sign, at a distance of 3 inches from the door, will not be hit by the opening door.

So much for the letter of the law. You are probably asking yourself right now, "What is grade 2 Braille?" and "Why are we doing this?" The Braille alphabet is made up of one cell for each letter of the alphabet. Each cell can have up to six dots, resembling a domino. When Braille is printed or embossed on the page, it takes up more space than printed words, and, of course, you can't write anything on the back side of a page. Consequently, Braille takes up a lot of space. A set of 189 abbreviations and contractions are used in Braille for common words and word endings which reduces the space and reading time needed for Braille text. This abbreviated version of the language is called grade 2 Braille.

But why Braille? In a population of nearly 45,000 students, faculty, and staff at Arizona State University (ASU), there are only eleven people who read Braille. These amazing people find their way around campus pretty well without room numbers, and they already know where the restrooms, elevators, and stairs are. Wouldn't it be cheaper to orient each student to the campus as we have been doing in the past? Why do they need Braille numbers and labels if they don't even use them?

I have put these questions to the wise and talented individual on our campus who works with all of the vision-impaired students through our campus Disabled Student Resources (DSR) Center. His answer was twofold: first, when sighted students have a class in 101 Murdoch Hall, they follow maps or instructions to get there, and as they enter the room, they can look above the door to see that the room they are entering

is, indeed, numbered 101. Blind students do not have this assurance. They will not know where they are unless they ask someone or unless someone from DSR affixes a Braille label on the door frame, hoping that no one peels it off. So the numbering of rooms in Braille will give blind people the assurance that they have reached their destination, something sighted individuals have long taken for granted.

The second part of the answer is more involved, and more fascinating. The reason that there are so few Braille readers on our campus is a consequence of changes in technology and educational theory. Twenty-five years ago, with the advent of the cassette tape recorder, there was a shift in the education of blind students—it became much easier to record books for the blind than it was to reproduce books in Braille. Simple equipment made it easier for readers and listeners. The immediate comprehension of the recorded word was favored over the tedious process of learning to read Braille, and research showed that students learned as well by tapes as they did by reading Braille.

But recent research comparing the retention of what is learned by reading Braille versus retention of information learned by listening shows Braille to be far superior. Tapes are linear; you can't go back and review certain bits of information. It's difficult to follow instructions or procedures on tape. And how can you learn to write?

In addition to the change in educational theory, there is also a change in technology. Optical scanners can now be used to convert text into Braille with a minimum of time and effort. At ASU any student who needs a text or reading book converted into Braille can have it done overnight by DSR staff. In a process that's similar to photocopying, the book is scanned, the information goes through a computer program, and the pages are reproduced in Braille by an embosser driven by the computer. So now Braille is easier to produce than recorded tapes, a situation which is helping to usher in a revival of Braille.

Of the blind adult population in the United States today, 70 percent are unemployed. Of those who are gainfully employed, 85 percent read Braille. These individuals have the highest education, are the most successful, and are also the most vocal on issues affecting the blind population. These are the people who are fighting for a revival of Braille and who caused the government to include Braille requirements in the ADA legislation.

Returning to library signage, here are some suggestions for new signs that will help everyone:

Be careful that floor plans on every floor are oriented correctly, not just mass produced and hung upside down or sideways. Floor plans can be done with computer-aided design programs. They can be easily updated on disk and printed by a laser printer. Photocopy machines can greatly enlarge the floor plans, which can be hung in large picture frames (using non-glare glass) opposite elevators or stairs on every floor.

People shouldn't have to go back to the entrance to find out which floor they need to visit next. Again, use computer software to update the building directory, enlarge the printout by photocopying, and provide a directory in another large picture frame next to the floor plans on every floor.

People can get turned around very easily in massive, open library stacks. Emergency exit signs will lead them to fire stairs when they really want to find the elevator or the front door. Walk through your library and see where you may need to place signs leading to stairs or elevators.

Changing Signage

We now move to changes in signs that are required by the ADA. To begin with, all permanent, directional, and identification signs are required to have a non-glare finish and sharp contrast between the colors of the letters and background.

The typeface, or font, of the lettering must be sans serif or simple serif and have a width-to-height proportion of 3:5 to 1:1, a stroke width-to-height ratio of 1:5 to 1:10. That is as complicated as it sounds, but the Society of Environmental Graphic Designers has simplified this requirement by providing a list of acceptable type fonts. The list includes Helvetica, Century Schoolbook, Times, Palatino, and several others that are commonly used. (Incidentally, Helvetica Medium is the easiest type to read tactilely.)

If you don't have a good contrast between the letters and the backgrounds, or if the finish is shiny, or if the type is tall and skinny or short and fat, you will have to repaint or re-letter your signs. Before you do, here's another requirement to keep in mind: All overhead signs must have letters 3 inches high, and the signs must be hung with a minimum clearance of 80 inches. Practically speaking, one line of 3-inch type,

with the appropriate 3-inch margins above and below, will come to 9 inches, plus 80 inches' clearance, and a minimum of 1 inch for hardware, or 90 inches. Two lines of type will require 94½ to 96 inches, or an eight-foot ceiling. In other words, you can't have more than two lines of type on an overhead sign if you have eight-foot ceilings. So you must practice word economy without confusing people.

Since you will probably end up changing some signs, here are more suggestions that aren't required but will really help all users of your library:

Make all the signs look alike. Signs that all have the same colors and type style will come to be recognized by library users, who will then look for them when they need information.

Place signs at decision points. Studies have shown that people look for information only at the location where a decision is to be made. Signs that aren't in the right places will be ignored.

Use larger type where possible. Labels on file cabinet drawers, periodical shelves, and some end ranges were made in the past using a typewriter. Make these labels easier to read by redoing them on a computer word processing program: scale up the size of the font and switch to bold Helvetica to make them as readable as possible from the farthest distance. The new labels will be easier to read, and will lessen the need to stoop or bend over to see what is written below eye level.

Get rid of the glare. A big complaint by the visually impaired students at ASU is glare, causing signs to be more difficult to read. Unfortunately, all directories are considered "temporary" by the ADA, and so every glassy-faced directory in the library and elsewhere is exempt from the matte finish requirement. It is possible in some cases to replace glass or acrylic sheets with non-glare, matte finish materials. We intend to replace the fronts on all our library directories, but we won't get any help from the campus ADA team, since this is not a requirement for compliance with ADA. In the future, avoid purchasing any sign holders, bulletin board cases, picture frames, or directories that have a glare finish.

If you have clear, shiny protective covers over labels on range finders, periodical shelves, file cabinet drawers, or elsewhere, look to see if there is a glare problem. Consider replacing the covers with matte finish material or removing them altogether.

Removing Signage

Now that you've added signs and changed others to comply with ADA, it's time to get rid of some signs. The only ones you *must* get rid of are the ones that you couldn't change to meet ADA requirements.

After you've disposed of ADA–induced obsolescence, there is something you can do that will greatly help all who enter your library. *Get rid of the sign clutter.* Let go. The fewer signs, the better. If you overwhelm people with too many signs, they won't read any of them. Research has shown that people spend about eight seconds reading a sign, and they prefer to read a sign and make a decision while still moving rather than stopping to read. So if they aren't absolutely necessary, and especially if they are not working to produce the desired results, take the signs down. You will find that the library is neater and more efficient with the new signage I've just recommended, and less stressful with all with the signage clutter removed.

Conclusion

In closing, I would like to reflect on the spirit of ADA, the law requiring the removal of barriers to the disabled. The ADA addresses the determined needs of the mobility and sight-impaired in our country, but not the undetermined needs of an estimated 20 percent of the population having some form of disability. No one has written laws or produced guidelines for us to follow to make the removal of all barriers a reality. And yet we are charged with accomplishing this task.

The ADA can be seen as flexible or vague, depending on your degree of optimism. It has been said that the only way to prove you are in compliance is to win a lawsuit brought against you, and the ADA has been called the "Lawyers' Full Employment Act." To succeed with the "must do" tasks in library signage, prioritize the signage changes based on the extent of the changes needed and the cost involved. Build these priorities into your ongoing maintenance and construction plans. Follow through and document the changes, both for legal purposes and to plan for future facilities costs.

Keep in touch with representatives of the groups of disabled users you are trying to help. Find out what they need or want, and tell them what you are doing or intend to do. Keep communication open. There should not be any surprises. At ASU there have been about half a dozen complaints filed against the University (none regarding the library), all of which were corrected satisfactorily so the suits were dropped. That is how the ADA is intended to work. The government wants people to step forward and identify themselves and their needs so that they can be addressed.

Back to the "can do" part of library signage. Increase your awareness of the problems associated with disabilities.

> Get to know the situations confronting the disabled. Observe them, talk to them, listen to them. Subscribe to an online bulletin board list and read their comments and complaints; ask questions.

> Become more aware of different kinds of disabilities. You're in the library all day. Look up relevant materials and read about them. Share with others what you've learned.

> Become more aware of issues facing the disabled. Did you know that the move toward graphics interfaces on computers, such as Macintosh and Windows, is a threat to blind users who type and read by touching Braille keys? Did you know about the revival of Braille? These issues have implications for library management and decision making.

No matter what your job is in the library, no matter what your responsibility is for ADA compliance, you've probably come to realize by now that this legislation has created a process, not a project. We can work at it and make progress, but we will never finish bringing our libraries into compliance. And that is as it should be. We will never finish building our library collections or checking out books or answering reference questions. And we will never finish adapting our libraries to meet the needs of all users.

Selected Bibliography

Basic How-to Guides

Eastman Kodak Company, Human Factors Section, Health, Safety, and Human Factors Laboratory.

Workplace, Equipment, and Environmental Design and Information Transfer. v. 1. *Ergonomic Design for People at Work.* Belmont, Calif.: Lifetime Learning Publication, 1983.

"New Directions for Signage: Clear, Concise Signage Is Key to Building Aesthetics and Functionality." *Buildings* 83 (March 1989): 72–73.

Good Old Texts, Parts of Which Are Still Useful

Pollet, Dorothy and Peter C. Haskell, eds. *Sign Systems for Libraries: Solving the Wayfinding Problem.* New York: R. R. Bowker, 1979.

Reynolds, Linda and Stephen Barrett. *Signs and Guiding for Libraries.* London: Bingley, 1981.

Spencer, Herbert and Linda Reynolds. *Directional Signing and Labelling in Libraries and Museums: A Review of Current Theory and Practice.* London: Royal College of Art, Readability of Print Research Unit, 1977.

Research Studies You Can Understand

Eaton, Gail. "Wayfinding in the Library: Book Searches and Route Uncertainty." *RQ* 30 (Summer 1991): 519–527.

———, Michael Vocino, and Melanie Taylor. "Evaluating Signs in a University Library." *Collection Development* 16 (1992): 81–101.

O'Neil, Michael J. "Effects of Signage and Floor Plan Configuration on Wayfinding Accuracy. *Environment and Behavior* 23 (September 1991): 553–574.

Seemingly Unrelated But Helpful Information

Cubberly, Carol W. "Write Procedures That Work." *Library Journal* 116 (September 15, 1991): 42–45.

Matthew, Diane L. "The Scientific Poster: Guidelines for Effective Visual Communication." *Technical Communication* 37 (August 1990): 225–232.

Thought-Provoking Background Material

Arthur, Paul and Romedi Passini. *Wayfinding: People, Signs, and Architecture.* New York: McGraw-Hill, 1992.

Berger, Arthur Asa. *Seeing Is Believing: An Introduction to Visual Communication.* Mountain View, Calif.: Mayfield, 1989.

———. *Signs in Contemporary Culture: An Introduction to Semiotics.* New York: Longman, 1984.

Morgan, John and Peter Welton. *See What I Mean?: An Introduction to Visual Communication.* 2nd ed. London: Edward Arnold, 1992.

Tufte, Edward R. *Envisioning Information.* Cheshire, Conn.: Graphics Pr., 1990.

———. *The Visual Display of Quantitative Information.* Cheshire, Conn.: Graphics Pr., 1983.

Wileman, Ralph E. *Exercises in Visual Thinking.* New York: Hastings House, 1980.

Wolf, Henry. *Visual Thinking: Methods for Making Images Memorable.* New York: American Showcase, 1988.

Wurman, Richard Saul. *Information Anxiety.* New York: Doubleday, 1989.

ADA and Signage

Ethridge, Kenneth A. "Signs of Change." *Construction Specifier* 45 (August 1992): 84–93.

Finke, Gail. "Tactful and Tactile: *Identity's* Continuing Coverage of the Americans with Disabilities Act." *Identity* 5 (Summer 1992): 28–32.

Goldsmith, Marianne. "Legal Side." *Step-by-Step Graphics* 8 (September 1992): 28–37.

"Special: Signs for ADA." *Identity* 5 (Spring 1992): 28B-46.

U.S. Department of Justice, Equal Employment Opportunity Commission. *Americans with Disabilities Handbook.* Washington, D.C.: GPO, 1992.

CHAPTER NINE

Safety and Security Considerations

Rachel MacLachlan

Before we begin I have a few questions:

When staying in a hotel, how many of you make sure that your room key is somewhere where you could find it if you needed it in a hurry in the middle of the night?

How many of you know where the nearest fire extinguisher is, in relation to the place where you usually sit at work?

How many of you know CPR or the Heimlich maneuver?

The Red Cross recommends that you renew your CPR certification every two years. How many of you have a current certificate?

How many of you have stopped to think about the safest place to go if there were an earthquake right now?

You should know where your room keys are because in the event of a fire or other emergency evacu-

Rachel MacLachlan is director of security at San Francisco Public Library. She has been involved in law enforcement and security since entering the San Francisco Police Academy in 1982. She earned a master's degree from the School of Library and Information Studies at the University of California, Berkeley, in 1991.

ation you may want to return to your room and you don't want to be locked out. In the event of a fire your room is often the safest place to be. There is probably something in your room describing steps to take in case of a fire. Every year people are killed in hotel fires; knowing what to do could save your life.

The point of this exercise is to demonstrate how easy it is to not think about emergency preparedness. Safety awareness and emergency preparedness are not things that we can think about once a year at training sessions—they are active and ongoing processes.

While most of the technical requirements of the Uniform Federal Accessibility Standards (UFAS) and the Americans with Disabilities Act Accessibility Guidelines (ADAAG) are concerned to some degree with safety, actively thinking about safety and emergency preparedness is essential if we are going to take that step beyond just complying with the law. And on this issue I think we want to go the extra step. If someone comes to one of our facilities and discovers that a disability means they can't use one of our services, the frustrated user may feel unwelcome or may sue, but if we fail to anticipate a safety or emergency preparedness problem, the user may be injured or dead.

A library in the San Francisco area recently had a safety problem brought to its attention the hard way. I'm sure many libraries have ramps that were designed for book trucks rather than for wheelchairs. This library had a ramp running down a short flight of stairs to a relatively unused area. A patron took his wheelchair down the short ramp safely but when he tried to come back up, the chair flipped over backwards—he ended up with a fractured spine. The ramp was more than 300 percent steeper than UFAS allows, and there was no handrail. Some people have mentioned difficulties convincing those who control the purse strings to fund ADA compliance. If the possibility of a broken back doesn't concern them, perhaps the size of the lawsuit would.

Accessibility Audit

Merely complying with ADA may not be enough, but is a good place start. One of the first steps should be to conduct an accessibility audit. The staff who walked past the ramp on a daily basis, including those who were responsible for the safety of the facility, had simply never thought about that ramp and why it was there. This is not surprising. Until we are educated, until we start thinking about accessibility, these issues don't come to mind, particularly when potential problems are part of our daily environment. An accessibility audit might well have prevented an injury and a lawsuit in this situation. This example points to the urgency of moving ahead with audits. There are a number of workbooks available that take one through an audit step by step. I recommend *Surveying Public Libraries for the ADA* by J. B. Black, et al., published by the Florida State Library in 1992.

I emphasize, however, that you do not have to conduct a formal audit to locate and fix obvious problems. Solutions to safety hazards may be relatively simple. The offending ramp that flipped the wheelchair was not a permanent part of the building. A library administrator and one other staff member removed it in ten minutes—eight minutes locating and advising the affected department head, two minutes dragging the ramp to an out-of-the-way location.

Technical Requirements

Before reviewing a few of the most common safety problems, I will briefly explain the technical standards that are mandated by the ADA. At present there are two different sets of standards in use—the Uniform Federal Accessibility Standards (UFAS) and the Americans with Disabilities Act Accessibility Guidelines (ADAAG). If your library falls under Title III of the ADA (covering non-governmental places of public accommodation), you are required to follow the ADAAG. Most of you, however, are Title II entities, and as such have the choice as to which standard you will follow. The UFAS is useful for many institutions because it contains specific guidelines for places such as jails and hazardous materials facilities, but it is somewhat less stringent and less comprehensive than the ADAAG. As these two standards are eventually going to be combined into one uniform standard, and for your general protection, I would suggest that you follow the ADAAG. Unless specified otherwise, those are the standards I will be describing.

Ramps are potential problem areas. The general rule for ramps is that they should not have a slope of more than 1:12. This is actually a fairly simple rule. Your ramp needs a foot of length for every inch of vertical rise. If the elevation change is 2 feet, your ramp needs to be 24 feet long. This rule is strict for new construction. In existing buildings a ramp may have a 1:10 ratio if the rise is less than 6 inches and a 1:8 ratio if the rise is less than 3 inches. The ramp may not have a cross slope of more than 1:50. In other words, it may not slope noticeably to one side. The maximum rise for a single ramp without landings is 36 inches. If the rise is greater than 6 inches or the ramp is more than 72 inches long, it must have handrails on both sides. These rails must be continuous, be from 34 to 38 inches above the ramp, and be at least 1½ inches out from any walls on either side. If you have ramps in your facility that are significantly out of compliance with these standards, they are a potential safety hazard. If they cannot be repaired, you might consider whether it is possible to block them off or at least post signs advising users that they are not intended to be used by wheelchairs. Of course you are then acknowledging that it is not an accessible route.

Poor walking surfaces are another problem. ADAAG calls for ground and floor surfaces to be "stable, firm . . . and slip resistant." Any rise of more than ¼ inch must have an edge treatment. If the rise is less than ½ inch it must have a beveled 1:2 slope. If the rise is greater than ½ inch you must install a ramp. Carpets must be attached to the floor and may not have pile thicker than ½ inch. The holes in floor gratings may not be more than ½ inch wide in their narrow dimension, and the long dimension must be parallel to the direction of travel. Tripping caused by non-compliance with these sections is probably one of the most common safety hazards. A likely problem area is in library children's departments. Many places use loose carpet squares and other small carpets for children to sit on. One of my first hands-on experiences with electric wheelchair repair came in trying to disentangle a patron from a throw rug in our children's department.

Objects that protrude into passageways are another problem. Even sighted people sometimes walk into phone booths, fire extinguishers, and other items that protrude from the walls, but blind people may have no way of avoiding them. The most serious problems are objects that do not reach to ground level. People using canes can detect an object at or near ground level before they bump into it. If the bottom edge of an object is more than 27 inches but less than 80 inches above the ground, ADAAG prohibits these items from protruding more than 4 inches into a passageway. Fire extinguishers, standpipes, and display cases may all be problems. A "low-tech" fix is to place a chair or some other item that is detectable at ground level in front of the protruding object. Just make sure that such an object doesn't stick so far out into the pathway as to impinge on the general rule that an accessible pathway should be at least 36 inches wide. Also make sure that there are at least 80 inches of headroom along all accessible pathways.

Minor safety hazards that are mostly an annoyance for the able-bodied become potentially serious problems for our disabled staff and patrons—doors that are heavy and hard to open, elevator doors that close too quickly. Anything that is a safety problem for everyone may be a much more serious problem for someone with a disability. Simply making sure that a building is in compliance with general rules of safety is an excellent step toward making it accessible, and everyone benefits, not just those of us with disabilities.

Tactile Warnings

Increased awareness of the needs of the disabled has led to the creation of new products, some of which are particularly related to safety. Tactile or detectable warnings are one example. Most commonly in use are tiles with large rounded bumps that are placed on the floor surface next to dangerous areas such as the edge of a railroad platform. The other most common type is texturing on a door handle that alerts someone before they enter a room that there is hazardous material or dangerous equipment inside; this latter type is re-

quired for facilities that are following the UFAS. The ADAAG originally required a number of tactile warnings, but recently all such requirements were suspended pending further review. This underscores a fact that we all need to keep in mind—the UFAS and the ADAAG are living documents. Much of the technology is new or is being used in new ways. Solutions that work well in one setting may not work well in others, and experts may disagree about what works. Tactile warnings on the ground had been used with considerable success in California and Florida. But after they were incorporated into the ADAAG, concerns were raised that not enough was known about how they performed in snow and ice. There have also been concerns that if they are used too much they lose their effectiveness. This does not mean that tactile warnings should not be used in the interim if one keeps those concerns in mind. It is likely that they will be required in final technical standards and can be an effective way of alerting people to particular dangers.

Book Detection Systems

A number of people have asked about book detection systems. The ADAAG specifically mentions them. Simply put, they must meet the same standards required in any other part of an accessible route. Many systems have a raised floor plate. The standards for floor surfaces apply. If the plate is less than ½ inch thick you can bevel the edges. If it is thicker you need a short ramp. The width of the aisle must be 36 inches, except that it may narrow to 32 inches for a distance of not more than 24 inches. This is where the most serious problems arise—many older gates are less than 36 inches wide.

If you have a radio frequency system, such as Checkpoint, you are probably okay. These systems are usually less than 24 inches deep, and as long as your aisle is 32 inches wide, you are fine. They have fewer problems working at wider aisle widths than the electromagnetic systems, so their aisles often were originally built wider. Electromagnetic systems don't work as well at wider distances. All the major manufacturers are now making systems that will work at 36 inches or wider, but older systems may be a problem. Not only do they have to be able to function at those widths, they have to be modified by the replacement of the base plates.

Most of the older electromagnetic systems in libraries were made by 3M, so let me go over the different 3M models. The 1850 system is the one that has the white lattice on one side of the aisle and the square post on the other. This system cannot be modified and must be replaced. The 1350 systems, which were installed before 1972 and have cloth on the sides, must also be replaced. The 1355, 1360, and 1365 systems, however, can be modified for approximately $500 to $800. It is important to keep in mind that these will not work quite as well as they did before widening. So if your system is older, you may want to replace it.

I have also been asked about whether book detection systems can continue to have locking gates. The answer is yes, but there are some accessibility issues which must be addressed. They need to meet the standards for doors in terms of clearance and amount of force required for opening. The system also needs a flashing light to alert hearing-impaired users that the alarm has sounded. If you do nothing else, ensure that every locking gate has a sign that warns users that the gate will lock if the alarm sounds. This benefits everybody and might alert a deaf patron to approach the gate with caution. Also, some portion of the gate should be low enough to be detectable to a person using a cane. Locking gates are extremely useful in certain settings, and with these considerations in mind it is quite possible to make them fully accessible.

Emergency Preparedness

The ADAAG and the UFAS both specifically emphasize the importance of every building having an emergency management plan that addresses the needs of the disabled. Most facilities don't even have good emergency management plans for the able-bodied, let alone plans that give consideration to the special needs and vulnerabilities of the disabled. It is my hope that the ADA will prompt administrators to think more concretely about this issue.

The key to any emergency management plan is prevention. As prevention has to be an ongoing process, and because our environments generally aren't that dangerous, it often falls by the wayside. We recently had a potentially serious incident that was caused by an electrical problem that several staff members were aware of, but everyone assumed someone else had reported it. Institutions frequently put barriers in the way of reporting safety problems. Requests for repairs can only be made on special forms or only certain people are allowed to contact the people who are in a position to do something. It must be made easy for any staff member to report a concern to someone who is in a position to investigate and address the

problem quickly, and people need to be encouraged rather than punished for doing so.

Alarm Systems

The ADAAG has a number of specific technical requirements in the area of emergency management. Audible alarms must be set to sound at least 15 decibels above ambient noise in the area. Varying or intermittent tones are recommended over steady tones. Visual alarms tied to the building alarm system are now required in every general use area, including restrooms and staff lounges, and in any offices frequently used by hearing-impaired staff. They must be placed at least 80 inches above the floor and 6 inches below the ceiling. Visual alarms flash a powerful white strobe light, the strength and speed of which are exactly specified in the ADAAG. Some details of these specifications may be subject to change because of the discovery that, in some situations, visual alarms cause seizures in people subject to light-induced epilepsy. This is another example of why you need to be alert for changes in the ADAAG. In this case, the details are very technical and the companies selling the alarms should be finding this out for you.

Eventually new alarm systems will be installed, but there are some low-tech steps that you can take immediately that will help you alert disabled staff and patrons to evacuate. Bells or alarms with intermittent or oscillating tones are more audible to people who are hearing-impaired. If your alarms are rung manually, arrange to have them rung intermittently. If they are automatic it may be possible to modify them to sound something other than a constant tone. You also can create a sort of visual alarm by flashing the ceiling lights. Obviously, this is less effective in a brightly lit room, but even small changes in lighting might alert someone accustomed to relying on visual cues. Another way to alert people visually is by carrying signs. At our library we have made large signs that say, "There is an emergency. Please leave the building now." Staff checking the building carry these signs with them. Vibrating pagers are a good solution for reaching deaf staff members working in isolated parts of the building. Every one of these techniques requires staff training, cooperation, and scheduled practice drills.

Once people are aware that they need to leave, they must be able to find their way out. Proper emergency signage may be especially necessary for those who may not be getting the visual or auditory cues to help them find an exit. Talking emergency signs are now on the market which audibly direct people toward an exit. A light- or dark-colored pathway in the carpet or floor tile can help people with low vision find an exit. Required signage should be in place, and the lights in emergency exit signs should be checked and repaired regularly.

You may have noticed signs on subways or trains telling you that in an evacuation wheelchairs should be left behind. Certainly in many cases that may be the best solution, but wheelchairs are more than just furniture. They need to be viewed as an extension of their users' bodies, and some persons may die if they are removed from their wheelchairs under the wrong circumstances. In our planning we must recognize that it is not always desirable or possible to evacuate someone without their wheelchair. More importantly, even in an evacuation we must be prepared to listen to the disabled people we are trying to assist.

The ADAAG requires areas of rescue assistance in new multi-story buildings not having supervised automatic sprinkler systems. These areas, also known as areas of refuge, are predesignated and prepared sites where people can go to await fire department rescue. They must be in a fire-resistant area of the building; they must be large enough to hold two wheelchairs, and they must have a two-way communication system that allows users to tell rescuers where they are, and that enables rescuers to let them know that help is on the way. The areas must be accessible, well marked, and close to fire stairs that are wide enough for a person to be carried out in a wheelchair. The ADAAG now also recommends that building elevators have an independent emergency power source that would enable firefighters to evacuate people in wheelchairs even if the building power is out. Many emergency management experts have reservations about areas of rescue assistance and it is the hope of many fire professionals that, since they are not required for buildings with sprinkler systems, the primary result of this requirement will be many more buildings with sprinklers. However, these rescue areas are still better than nothing, and in some cases it may not be all that difficult to incorporate them into existing buildings. If your buildings do not have these features, a possibility is to train some of your stronger staff members to carry someone down the stairs in a wheelchair.

Preparedness

The best building design and the best equipment won't do much if your staff is unprepared. Planning and training are critical elements of emergency preparedness. The planning process must include people with disabilities. In particular, the needs of disabled staff members must be anticipated and addressed. But planning is useless if it only leads to dusty emergency manuals sitting on dustier shelves. At least some staff members will probably need special training for their expected tasks—carrying someone in a wheelchair, for instance, may not be possible if you don't know how to do it. But even if no special training is required, it is critical that every staff member knows what to do in an emergency.

I cannot overemphasize the importance of drills. With sufficient practice it is far more likely that staff will remain calm under the stress of a real emergency. This could save the life of a deaf page working in a remote stack who is depending on someone to remember to call him on his vibrating pager. It is very important that some drills be unannounced. The other major reason for drills is that they help expose problems with your procedures, and many of those problems won't show up on an announced drill. I am extremely grateful that it was not an actual emergency that demonstrated that our procedures for evacuating deaf staff members were inadequate.

Conclusion

Our existing facilities inevitably pose many obstacles to providing a safe environment for our staff and patrons with disabilities. Particularly if we have new facilities planned for the future, the temptation may be to just delay dealing with the problems. But this is neither necessary nor appropriate. Many problems are easily addressed; others are too urgent to wait for new buildings. If serious or easily addressed problems are obvious, start working on them now. If accessibility audits have not yet been done, they should be completed as additional problems will certainly be brought to light. Once the audit is complete, I urge you to look closely at the issues that affect the safety of your staff and patrons.

A risk assessment model can be a very useful tool for determining how to focus an institution's limited resources for ADA compliance. Using this model, the probability that a safety problem will lead to an injury and the severity of that injury are both estimated to establish priorities. In its simplest form, this leads to a matrix with four possibilities:

high probability of injury; death or severe injury is possible;

high probability of injury; injuries are likely to be minor;

low probability of injury; death or severe injury is possible; and

low probability of injury; injuries are likely to be minor.

Intermediate estimates of probability and severity may be added creating a more detailed risk picture. These rankings can be used to prioritize responses. Only after this step is taken, should the cost be taken into consideration. The reality is that many institutions will not be able to address some moderately severe risks, but at least the administration will be alerted to the problem and it may be possible to take some partial steps and to plan for future repairs. If in the course of this process a very high-risk problem is identified for which there is no short term solution, I strongly suggest seeking legal advice as soon as possible. The priority for many people with disabilities is getting in the front door of a facility; I would argue that keeping people alive and uninjured is equally important.

The probable consequences of ignoring safety problems and failing to prepare for emergencies are injuries, possibly deaths, and almost certainly lawsuits. Only with new facilities will our institutions eliminate most of the structural and equipment problems addressed by the ADAAG, but we need to make a good faith effort to do what we can, now. Good emergency planning and adequate staff training cost relatively little and will make a tremendous difference, no matter how antiquated the building. If we take these steps, not only people with disabilities, but *every* person who uses our facilities will be safer.

CHAPTER TEN

The Good, the Bad, and the Ugly: Design Issues

Fred Kolflat and Robert Bruce Klug

Before we begin emphasizing a few more specifics of design, I'd like to stress that the purpose of mentioning federal lawsuits is not to increase anxiety levels. On the contrary, we want to emphasize that if you complete an audit, develop a plan, and begin working on compliance before being sued or forced to comply, you will ultimately incur less expense, even if you don't meet the deadlines.

We will walk through some examples of compliance and non-compliance. Some of the examples are things that have been done since the ADA has been passed. We use some examples from a building completed in 1989, before the ADA. A lot of things were done to try to comply with or exceed the standards without any knowledge of what the ADA standards would actually require.

Accessible Parking

Accessible parking should be as close to the entrance as possible. When you establish accessible parking, it must be marked by a sign on a post that is high enough to be visible above a parked vehicle. It should be noted that signs painted on the ground don't meet the ADA standards. In addition to visible signage, each parking space must be wide enough to enable someone in a wheelchair to maneuver out of the vehicle, and to a pedestrian walkway.

Accessible Entrances

Once you get out of your vehicle, if the entrance is not apparent you must have site signage to lead you to the accessible entrance. This is especially important when the accessible entrance is not in clear sight of the parking area.

There is a standard on adequate space in front of a door. You must have a space of 48 inches plus the length of the door in the open position, to provide a landing area to accommodate a wheelchair. Interior doors are limited to five pounds of force, but the exterior door is limited only by the building and fire codes. The ADA requires that all carpets and mats be fully secured to the floor on all sides. This requirement is not limited to accessible entrances. Fifty percent of the entrances must be accessible, but other standards must still be met even if the entrance is not considered accessible. A blind person or someone with a walker who can barely lift his or her feet off the ground may be able to use an entrance that is not wheelchair-accessible, but could have problems with loose floor mats. Foot-wipe material that is secured and flush with the threshold of the door on both sides is recommended. Electric doors that open out when you walk across the mat are not recommended because of the possibility that the door could hit somebody when it swings open; horizontally sliding doors are preferable. Roto-swing-type doors are available in a 3½-foot door size that gives a 38-inch clearance. The door has an offset pivot that is balanced so well that it requires very little effort to open.

Detectable Warnings

Detectable warnings on paved surfaces are required by the ADA to indicate hazards. The only approved design is truncated domes, ⁹⁄₁₀ inch in diameter, ¹⁄₁₀ inch high, and 2.35 inches on center, each way. They are to extend the full width and length of any curb cut. In situations where a driveway crosses a sidewalk, for example, the domes will alert a blind person to the possible danger.

The domes can be of any material, and they can be glued on, screwed in, or part of the concrete surface. Striations, grooves, rumble strips, and other variations do not meet ADA standards. The domes were selected because they are easily detected with a cane. Grooved surfaces cause problems because canes can get caught, and sometimes break. There are, however, also some problems with the domes. They are often slippery when wet, create problems with snow removal, and can cause problems for people who have mobility impairments and for women wearing high heels. Concerns about the domes should be addressed to the Justice Department, preferably through the blind or rehabilitative offices in your state, or relevant national organizations.

The use of the detectable warnings along the full length of the danger area is very important. One example of a dangerous situation is that of a sidewalk and a street merging together with no change in texture. A sighted person could see a painted line at the edge of the street, but a blind person would have no way of knowing where the street began. In another example, the sidewalk coming out of a building is concrete with a bit of a texture, and the driveway on the other side is plain finished concrete. In between are bollards marking the edge of the vehicular area, and a strip of concrete that has been raised up and has a rougher texture. This enables sight-impaired people coming out of the building to know exactly when they've reached the street. The angle at the edge of the raised

concrete is higher than the ADA requires, but there have been no problems with people in wheelchairs negotiating the bump.

Ramps and Stairs

The ADA has specific requirements for ramps. When they were being developed, there was considerable controversy on the appropriate slant for ramps. A 1:12-pitch ramp was negotiated. Unfortunately, only about 50 percent of people in wheelchairs can actually climb such a ramp in a wheelchair without assistance. Ramps must have handrails and a landing at least five feet long for every 30 vertical inches. Where it ends, the sidewalk should be level.

In addition to ramp requirements, there are ADA requirements for stairs. Elimination of stairs in favor of ramps is not advised. People with some types of mobility impairment may have more difficulty negotiating ramps than climbing properly designed stairs. Stairs must have 11 inches of clear tread. That means that, from the front edge of the nosing above to the nosing of the tread on the lower tread, there should be 11 inches clear. This is one item that will force many to use the "undue burden" clause. If you're in a building that is ten stories high and every tread in your building is 10½ inches long, you can't add ½ inch to each tread or you'll exceed the space that's available for the stairs in the building. Open risers are not permitted.

Lavatories

One way of making lavatories accessible is to eliminate doors by constructing an S-shaped entrance. Sinks should have adequate knee space for someone in a wheelchair. Water fountains, towel dispensers, and hand dryers should be installed at wheelchair height as well as regular height to accommodate people who have trouble stooping. Trash disposals should be low enough to reach from a wheelchair.

Service Desks

Any counter or transaction top must have at least one section that is 36 inches wide and not higher than 36 inches off the floor. In the interim, until you are able to alter or install a new service desk, put up a sign indicating how someone who is disabled can get assistance at another location. If someone is checking out a book and they have to sign their name or write something, you must have a space that is not higher than 34 inches. You also need to provide knee space, at least 19 inches deep, 27 inches high, and 30 inches wide, so that a wheelchair can fit under it. If all a patron has to do is set the book on the counter and then you take care of everything, 36 inches is adequate.

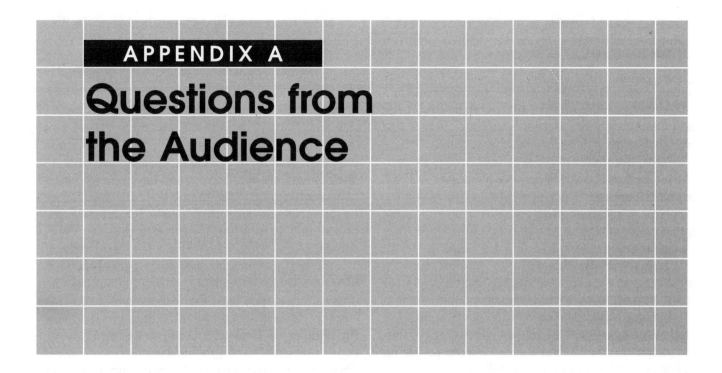

Questions from the Audience

How do you measure how much force is needed to pull on a door?

You need a very highly calibrated fish scale—a small handheld device that has a hook at the end of it which fishermen carry in their tackle box. Look for one that accommodates up to about twenty-five pounds. The door pull can't exceed five pounds on an interior door. Most building codes set the limits for exterior doors—the ADA sets the hold on exterior doors to be equal to whatever the building code requires, which is usually fifteen pounds. So, you do want to check your exterior doors. If you have one that takes twenty-five pounds' force to open, then you must have the door adjusted. Oftentimes when it's more than fifteen pounds it's because the door is sticking.

We have loose mats that we put down on a marble floor to help prevent people from slipping in wet weather, yet they do cause problems for individuals with disabilities. Does anyone have any recommendations for an alternative method of preventing slipping on this kind of floor?

Carborundum strips. I have another suggestion on the marble floor. At Arizona State University one of the buildings had that problem, particularly with a staircase. They solved the problem by sandblasting grids in the area that was affected.

You raised a question about stack heights, and if I understand correctly, the law doesn't actually specify. It says stack heights can be unrestricted, but what does that mean? If you're a Title II institution and have to provide program access, does that really mean that someone has to be available to get books off the shelf?

At Northeastern we provide an on-request retrieval service so that we can make the materials accessible. We don't have a loaner reaching mechanism that we hand out, although I suppose that could be another way of doing it. But our circulation department staff will retrieve material that can't be reached upon request.

But that's not very equalizing because it takes away the browsing factor which other people have. That's a concern that has been mentioned by some of the staff and patrons in my public library.

There's another concern too—the "reasonable accommodation" provision of the law. One of the things that we as space planners might be concerned about, although it may seem contrary to the general tenor of what we've been discussing today, is the cost of doing that. Probably the most expensive, or a very expensive, component of any building project is the space. If you have to lower the heights of all your stacks, that multiplies dramatically the number of square feet required to hold the same number of volumes. So providing a retrieval service is an efficient way of providing access to the program although it does not provide the same browsing capability.

In San Francisco, in the new facility that we are building, we plan to include lifts that accommodate either a wheelchair or a person, and that will lift the individual up to move along rows of books. Equipment like that is available to help address some of these concerns. But there's also the issue of bottom shelves. We have people on staff who have temporary and permanent disabilities which prevent them from bending. Appliances, such as mirrors that may make it possible for people to at least see the spines of those books, may be one solution.

Something else that you can consider doing is increasing the amount of display shelving in your stacks by putting a sloped shelf midway down a section of shelving; also, putting a little more effort into changing displays and having some browsing capability within the stacks. You then give more people an opportunity to see more of the collection.

Terry Foster of the Texas Rehabilitation Commission Library noted a few things that I think would be appropriate to mention. She runs a library that's mainly for people with disabilities, and she mentioned putting difficult-to-access books either in a special section, or making sure that they are shelved in such a way that individuals can get them off the shelf without having to ask for assistance. The other thing that she stressed is that librarians are probably in the most unique position of anyone in the country to take a proactive stance to assist in disseminating information, and to take a leadership role in helping people who have disabilities. I think that the videotape that the ALA [*People First*, Library Video Network, 1990] has produced is an excellent resource for just working on that "attitude, attitude, attitude."

Does anyone have comments or observations on handicapped access to publicly accessible, movable compact shelving, both electrical and mechanical? A lot of libraries have put in movable compact shelving that is now publicly accessible, not just for the staff. These are both electrically and manually operated. Does anyone have any observations on any special problems?

One problem is that typically the aisles are only 36 inches wide, the minimum aisle width when you're concerned about maximum capacity. So you must space your stack aisles so that when they are in an open position you have a wider aisle.

Many times compact shelving dead-ends against a wall. In that case, you need an even wider aisle. You'd have to have a five-foot-wide aisle in order for a wheelchair to turn around.

One of the things that was discussed yesterday was attitude. I suggest that you organize a workshop for staff and patrons in your library and invite people with disabilities to discuss what it's like being hearing-impaired, what it's like being in a wheelchair, what it's like being blind, etc. They would have a much better idea of what their disability is, and how your library facility accommodates their needs. I'm handicapped myself, and I think it's a great idea that everybody should follow.

We also recommend that every person spend at least one day in a wheelchair or on crutches; take an opportunity to spend one day with a blindfold on. You can experience firsthand what the difficulty is. One of the librarians at Gallaudet University pointed out recently that in the bibliographical instruction areas and library classrooms they need to set up either round or square tables so that everyone can see who is speaking. In a situation like this, with a panel facing the audience, if a question is asked and you respond, the person in the back who is hearing-impaired can't read lips and isn't able to participate fully in the discussions.

Someone else was telling me how difficult it is for a blind person to hear because those of us who are not blind or vision-impaired don't realize how much of our hearing is filtered out by our sight. We can filter out extraneous noise and conversations because we can see who is talking to us. Someone who is blind doesn't have that same ability to filter out the conversation. That's something that's very important to keep in mind at service desks when you are talking to someone. If there are a lot of conversations in the vicinity and you're talking to someone who has severe vision impairment, that person may not realize that you're talking to him or her.

I would like to emphasize staff awareness of these issues. When people have some experience talking to disabled people about their disabilities, they will feel more comfortable doing it in real world settings. For example, a hearing-impaired person may be able to hear better from one ear than the other, but may not feel that it's worth trying to tell you. But you can stop and ask if it would be easier if you speak to one side or the other. There are many ways in which, if we just take a moment to ask someone how we can help them to understand us better, it can make a world of difference. If your staff is made aware of some of these things, the degree of elimination of communication barriers is just remarkable.

One of the things that we do in workshops is try to make a day of it. We always invite our guest speaker to have lunch with us, without assigning seats. But it is a nice idea to assign your staff to mix with your speaker so that they have an opportunity to see each other on a person-to-person basis. One strategy that I always use when I start the sensitizing workshops is to demonstrate that a blind person's brain doesn't stop just because they're blind. I ask participants to imagine all the nights that they tried to fall asleep in a dark room, but all the day's activities kept going through their minds.

I'd like to add one more thing. I often use a simulation exercise with my students so they can appreciate that the guidelines don't cover everything. But I think it's very important for us to do some sort of debriefing because if you just put someone in a wheelchair or you just fuzz up their glasses or you just put earplugs on them, they start thinking in terms of the disability instead of the capability of our patrons. Most people say, "Oh my God, I'd hate to be blind, I couldn't do anything, I couldn't get across campus!" Well, people do. People with disabilities have a lot of abilities and I think we need to emphasize that because we overlook it a lot.

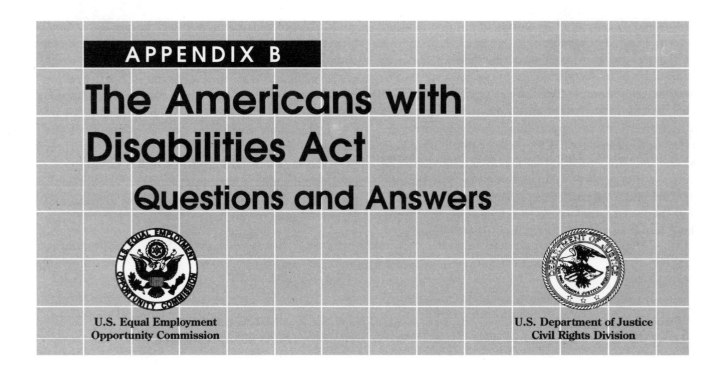

APPENDIX B

The Americans with Disabilities Act

Questions and Answers

**U.S. Equal Employment
Opportunity Commission**

**U.S. Department of Justice
Civil Rights Division**

Barriers to employment, transportation, public accommodations, public services, and telecommunications have imposed staggering economic and social costs on American society and have undermined our well-intentioned efforts to educate, rehabilitate, and employ individuals with disabilities. By breaking down these barriers, the Americans with Disabilities Act will enable society to benefit from the skills and talents of individuals with disabilities, will allow us all to gain from their increased purchasing power and ability to use it, and will lead to fuller, more productive lives for all Americans.

The Americans with Disabilities Act gives civil rights protections to individuals with disabilities similar to those provided to individuals on the basis of race, color, sex, national origin, age, and religion. It guarantees equal opportunity for individuals with disabilities in public accommodations, employment, transportation, State and local government services, and telecommunications.

Fair, swift, and effective enforcement of this landmark civil rights legislation is a high priority of the Federal Government. This booklet is designed to provide answers to some of the most often asked questions about the new law.

Employment

Q. What employers are covered by title I of the ADA, and when is the coverage effective?

A. The title I employment provisions apply to private employers, State and local governments, employment agencies, and labor unions. Employers with 25 or more employees are covered as of July 26, 1992. Employers with 15 or more employees will be covered two years later, beginning July 26, 1994.

Reprinted from *The Americans with Disabilities Act, Questions and Answers,* EEOC-BK-15, revised 1992.

Q. What practices and activities are covered by the employment non-discrimination requirements?

A. The ADA prohibits discrimination in all employment practices, including job application procedures, hiring, firing, advancement, compensation, training, and other terms, conditions, and privileges of employment. It applies to recruitment, advertising, tenure, layoff, leave, fringe benefits, and all other employment-related activities.

Q. Who is protected from employment discrimination?

A. Employment discrimination is prohibited against "qualified individuals with disabilities." This includes applicants for employment and employees. An individual is considered to have a "disability" if s/he has a physical or mental impairment that substantially limits one or more major life activities, has a record of such an impairment, or is regarded as having such an impairment. Persons discriminated against because they have a known association or relationship with an individual with a disability also are protected.

The first part of the definition makes clear that the ADA applies to persons who have impairments and that these must substantially limit major life activities such as seeing, hearing, speaking, walking, breathing, performing manual tasks, learning, caring for oneself, and working. An individual with epilepsy, paralysis, HIV infection, AIDS, a substantial hearing or visual impairment, mental retardation, or a specific learning disability is covered, but an individual with a minor, nonchronic condition of short duration, such as a sprain, broken limb, or the flu, generally would not be covered.

The second part of the definition protecting individuals with a record of a disability would cover, for example, a person who has recovered from cancer or mental illness.

The third part of the definition protects individuals who are regarded as having a substantially limiting impairment, even though they may not have such an impairment. For example, this provision would protect a qualified individual with a severe facial disfigurement from being denied employment because an employer feared the "negative reactions" of customers or co-workers.

Q. Who is a "qualified individual with a disability"?

A. A qualified individual with a disability is a person who meets legitimate skill, experience, education, or other requirements of an employment position that s/he holds or seeks, and who can perform the "essential functions" of the position with or without reasonable accommodation. Requiring the ability to perform "essential" functions assures that an individual with a disability will not be considered unqualified simply because of inability to perform marginal or incidental job functions. If the individual is qualified to perform essential job functions except for limitations caused by a disability, the employer must consider whether the individual could perform these functions with a reasonable accommodation. If a written job description has been prepared in advance of advertising or interviewing applicants for a job, this will be considered as evidence, although not conclusive evidence, of the essential functions of the job.

Q. Does an employer have to give preference to a qualified applicant with a disability over other applicants?

A. No. An employer is free to select the most qualified applicant available and to make decisions based on reasons unrelated to a disability. For example, suppose two persons apply for a job as a typist and an essential function of the job is to type 75 words per minute accurately. One applicant, an individual with a disability, who is provided with a reasonable accommodation for a typing test, types 50 words per minute; the other applicant who has no disability accurately types 75 words per minute. The employer can hire the applicant with the higher typing speed, if typing speed is needed for successful performance of the job.

Q. What limitations does the ADA impose on medical examinations and inquiries about disability?

A. An employer may not ask or require a job applicant to take a medical examination before making a job offer. It cannot make any preemployment inquiry about a disability or the nature or severity of a disability. An employer may, however, ask questions about the ability to perform specific job functions and may, with certain limitations, ask an individual with a disability to describe or demonstrate how s/he would perform these functions.

An employer may condition a job offer on the satisfactory result of a post-offer medical examination or medical inquiry if this is required of all entering employees in the same job category. A post-offer examination or inquiry does not have to be job-related and consistent with business necessity.

However, if an individual is not hired because a post-offer medical examination or inquiry reveals a disability, the reason(s) for not hiring must be job-related and consistent with business necessity. The employer also must show that no reasonable accommodation was available that would enable the individual to perform the essential job functions, or that accommodation would impose an undue hardship. A post-offer medical examination may disqualify an individual if the employer can demonstrate that the individual would pose a "direct threat" in the workplace (i.e., a significant risk of substantial harm to the health or safety of the individual or others) that cannot be eliminated or reduced below the "direct threat" level through reasonable accommodation. Such a disqualification is job-related and consistent with business necessity. A post-offer medical examination may not disqualify an individual with a disability who is currently able to perform essential job functions because of speculation that the disability may cause a risk of further injury.

After a person starts work, a medical examination or inquiry of an employee must be job-related and consistent with business necessity. Employers may conduct employee medical examinations where there is evidence of a job performance or safety problem, examinations required by other Federal laws, examinations to determine current "fitness" to perform a particular job, and voluntary examinations that are part of employee health programs.

Information from all medical examinations and inquiries must be kept apart from general personnel files as a separate, confidential medical record, available only under limited conditions.

Tests for illegal use of drugs are not medical examinations under the ADA and are not subject to the restrictions of such examinations.

Q. When can an employer ask an applicant to "self-identify" as having a disability?

A. Federal contractors and subcontractors who are covered by the affirmative action requirements of section 503 of the Rehabilitation Act of 1973 may invite individuals with disabilities to identify themselves on a job application form or by other pre-employment inquiry, to satisfy the section 503 affirmative action requirements. Employers who request such information must observe section 503 requirements regarding the manner in which such information is requested and used, and the procedures for maintaining such information as a separate, confidential record, apart from regular personnel records.

A pre-employment inquiry about a disability is allowed if required by another Federal law or regulation such as those applicable to disabled veterans and veterans of the Vietnam era. Pre-employment inquiries about disabilities may be necessary under such laws to identify applicants or clients with disabilities in order to provide them with required special services.

Q. Does the ADA require employers to develop written job descriptions?

A. No. The ADA does not require employers to develop or maintain job descriptions. However, a written job description that is prepared before advertising or interviewing applicants for a job will be considered as evidence along with other relevant factors. If an employer uses job descriptions, they should be reviewed to make sure they accurately reflect the actual functions of a job. A job description will be most helpful if it focuses on the results or outcome of a job function, not solely on the way it customarily is performed. A reasonable accommodation may enable a person with a disability to accomplish a job function in a manner that is different from the way an employee who is not disabled may accomplish the same function.

Q. What is "reasonable accommodation"?

A. Reasonable accommodation is any modification or adjustment to a job or the work environment that will enable a qualified applicant or employee with a disability to participate in the application process or to perform essential job functions. Reasonable accommodation also includes adjustments to assure that a qualified individual with a disability has rights and privileges in employment equal to those of employees without disabilities.

Q. What are some of the accommodations applicants and employees may need?

A. Examples of reasonable accommodation include making existing facilities used by employees readily accessible to and usable by an individual with a disability; restructuring a job; modifying work schedules; acquiring or modifying equipment; providing qualified readers or interpreters; or appropriately modifying examinations, training, or other programs. Reasonable accommodation also may include reassigning a current employee to a vacant position for which the individual is qualified, if the person is unable to do the original job because of a disability even with an accommodation. However, there is no obligation to find a position for an applicant who is not qualified for the position sought. Employers are not required to lower quality or quantity standards as an accommodation; nor are they obligated to provide personal use items such as glasses or hearing aids.

The decision as to the appropriate accommodation must be based on the particular facts of each case. In selecting the particular type of reasonable accommodation to provide, the principal test is that of effectiveness, i.e., whether the accommodation will provide an opportunity for a person with a disability to achieve the same level of performance and to enjoy benefits equal to those of an average, similarly situated person without a disability. However, the accommodation does not have to ensure equal results or provide exactly the same benefits.

Q. **When is an employer required to make a reasonable accommodation?**

A. An employer is only required to accommodate a "known" disability of a qualified applicant or employee. The requirement generally will be triggered by a request from an individual with a disability, who frequently will be able to suggest an appropriate accommodation. Accommodations must be made on an individual basis, because the nature and extent of a disabling condition and the requirements of a job will vary in each case. If the individual does not request an accommodation, the employer is not obligated to provide one except where an individual's known disability impairs his/her ability to know of, or effectively communicate a need for, an accommodation that is obvious to the employer. If a person with a disability requests, but cannot suggest, an appropriate accommodation, the employer and the individual should work together to identify one. There are also many public and private resources that can provide assistance without cost.

Q. **What are the limitations on the obligation to make a reasonable accommodation?**

A. The individual with a disability requiring the accommodation must be otherwise qualified, and the disability must be known to the employer. In addition, an employer is not required to make an accommodation if it would impose an "undue hardship" on the operation of the employer's business. "Undue hardship" is defined as an "action requiring significant difficulty or expense" when considered in light of a number of factors. These factors include the nature and cost of the accommodation in relation to the size, resources, nature, and structure of the employer's operation. Undue hardship is determined on a case-by-case basis. Where the facility making the accommodation is part of a larger entity, the structure and overall resources of the larger organization would be considered, as well as the financial and administrative relationship of the facility to the larger organization. In general, a larger employer with greater resources would be expected to make accommodations requiring greater effort or expense than would be required of a smaller employer with fewer resources.

If a particular accommodation would be an undue hardship, the employer must try to identify another accommodation that will not pose such a hardship. Also, if the cost of an accommodation would impose an undue hardship on the employer, the individual with a disability should be given the option of paying that portion of the cost which would constitute an undue hardship or providing the accommodation.

Q. Must an employer modify existing facilities to make them accessible?

A. The employer's obligation under title I is to provide access for an *individual* applicant to participate in the job application process, and for an *individual* employee with a disability to perform the essential functions of his/her job, including access to a building, to the work site, to needed equipment, and to all facilities used by employees. For example, if an employee lounge is located in a place inaccessible to an employee using a wheelchair, the lounge might be modified or relocated, or comparable facilities might be provided in a location that would enable the individual to take a break with co-workers. The employer must provide such access unless it would cause an undue hardship.

Under title I, an employer is not required to make its existing facilities accessible until a particular applicant or employee with a particular disability needs an accommodation, and then the modifications should meet that individual's work needs. However, employers should consider initiating changes that will provide general accessibility, particularly for job applicants, since it is likely that people with disabilities will be applying for jobs. The employer does not have to make changes to provide access in places or facilities that will not be used by that individual for employment-related activities or benefits.

Q. Can an employer be required to reallocate an essential function of a job to another employee as a reasonable accommodation?

A. No. An employer is not required to reallocate essential functions of a job as a reasonable accommodation.

Q. Can an employer be required to modify, adjust, or make other reasonable accommodations in the way a test is given to a qualified applicant or employee with a disability?

A. Yes. Accommodations may be needed to assure that tests or examinations measure the actual ability of an individual to perform job functions rather than reflect limitations caused by the disability. Tests should be given to people who have sensory, speaking, or manual impairments in a format that does not require the use of the impaired skill, unless it is a job-related skill that the test is designed to measure.

Q. Can an employer maintain existing production/performance standards for an employee with a disability?

A. An employer can hold employees with disabilities to the same standards of production/performance as other similarly situated employees without disabilities for performing essential job functions, with or without reasonable accommodation. An employer also can hold employees with disabilities to the same standards of production/performance as other employees regarding marginal functions unless the disability affects the person's ability to perform those marginal functions. If the ability to perform marginal functions is affected by the disability, the employer must provide some type of reasonable accommodation such as job restructuring but may not exclude an individual with a disability who is satisfactorily performing a job's essential functions.

Q. Can an employer establish specific attendance and leave policies?

A.   An employer can establish attendance and leave policies that are uniformly applied to all employees, regardless of disability, but may not refuse leave needed by an employee with a disability if other employees get such leave. An employer also may be required to make adjustments in leave policy as a reasonable accommodation. The employer is not obligated to provide additional paid leave, but accommodations may include leave flexibility and unpaid leave.

A uniformly applied leave policy does not violate the ADA because it has a more severe effect on an individual because of his/her disability. However, if an individual with a disability requests a modification of such a policy as a reasonable accommodation, an employer may be required to provide it, unless it would impose an undue hardship.

Q. Can an employer consider health and safety when deciding whether to hire an applicant or retain an employee with a disability?

A.   Yes. The ADA permits employers to establish qualification standards that will exclude individuals who pose a direct threat—i.e., a significant risk of substantial harm—to the health or safety of the individual or of others, if that risk cannot be eliminated or reduced below the level of a "direct threat" by reasonable accommodation. However, an employer may not simply assume that a threat exists; the employer must establish through objective, medically supportable methods that there is significant risk that substantial harm could occur in the workplace. By requiring employers to make individualized judgments based on reliable medical or other objective evidence rather than on generalizations, ignorance, fear, patronizing attitudes, or stereotypes, the ADA recognized the need to balance the interests of people with disabilities against the legitimate interests of employers in maintaining a safe workplace.

Q. Are applicants or employees who are currently illegally using drugs covered by the ADA?

A.   No. Individuals who currently engage in the illegal use of drugs are specifically excluded from the definition of a "qualified individual with a disability" protected by the ADA when the employer takes action on the basis of their drug use.

Q. Is testing for the illegal use of drugs permissible under the ADA?

A.   Yes. A test for the illegal use of drugs is not considered a medical examination under the ADA; therefore, employers may conduct such testing of applicants or employees and make employment decisions based on the results. The ADA does not encourage, prohibit, or authorize drug tests.

If the results of a drug test reveal the presence of a lawfully prescribed drug or other medical information, such information must be treated as a confidential medical record.

Q. **Are alcoholics covered by the ADA?**

A. Yes. While a current illegal user of drugs is not protected by the ADA if an employer acts on the basis of such use, a person who currently uses alcohol is not automatically denied protection. An alcoholic is a person with a disability and is protected by the ADA if s/he is qualified to perform the essential functions of the job. An employer may be required to provide an accommodation to an alcoholic. However, an employer can discipline, discharge, or deny employment to an alcoholic whose use of alcohol adversely affects job performance or conduct. An employer also may prohibit the use of alcohol in the workplace and can require that employees not be under the influence of alcohol.

Q. **Does the ADA override Federal and State health and safety laws?**

A. The ADA does not override health and safety requirements established under other Federal laws even if a standard adversely affects the employment of an individual with a disability. If a standard is required by another Federal law, an employer must comply with it and does not have to show that the standard is job related and consistent with business necessity. For example, employers must conform to health and safety requirements of the U.S. Occupational Safety and Health Administration. However, an employer still has the obligation under the ADA to consider whether there is a reasonable accommodation, consistent with the standards of other Federal laws, that will prevent exclusion of qualified individuals with disabilities who can perform jobs without violating the standards of those laws. If an employer can comply with both the ADA and another Federal law, then the employer must do so.

The ADA does not override State or local laws designed to protect public health and safety, except where such laws conflict with the ADA requirements. If there is a State or local law that would exclude an individual with a disability from a particular job or profession because of a health or safety risk, the employer still must assess whether a particular individual would pose a "direct threat" to health or safety under the ADA standard. If such a "direct threat" exists, the employer must consider whether it could be eliminated or reduced below the level of a "direct threat" by reasonable accommodation. An employer cannot rely on a State or local law that conflicts with ADA requirements as a defense to a charge of discrimination.

Q. **How does the ADA affect workers' compensation programs?**

A. Only injured workers who meet the ADA's definition of an "individual with a disability" will be considered disabled under the ADA, regardless of whether they satisfy criteria for receiving benefits under workers' compensation or other disability laws. A worker also must be "qualified" (with or without reasonable accommodation) to be protected by the ADA. Work-related injuries do not always cause physical or mental impairments severe enough to "substantially limit" a major life activity. Also, many on-the-job injuries cause temporary impairments which heal within a short period of time with little or no long-term or permanent impact. Therefore, many injured workers who qualify for benefits under workers' compensation or other disability benefits laws may not be protected by the ADA. An employer must consider work-related injuries on a case-by-case basis to know if a worker is protected by the ADA.

An employer may not inquire into an applicant's workers' compensation history before making a conditional offer of employment. After making a conditional job offer, an employer may inquire about a person's workers' compensation history in a medical inquiry or examination that is required of all applicants in the same job category. However, even after a conditional offer has been made, an employer cannot require a potential employee to have a medical examination because a response to a medical inquiry (as opposed to results from a medical examination) shows a previous on-the-job injury unless all applicants in the same job category are required to have an examination. Also, an employer may not base an employment decision on the speculation that an applicant may cause increased workers' compensation costs in the future. However, an employer may refuse to hire, or may discharge an individual who is not currently able to perform a job without posing a significant risk of substantial harm to the health or safety of the individual or others, if the risk cannot be eliminated or reduced by reasonable accommodation.

An employer may refuse to hire or may fire a person who knowingly provides a false answer to a lawful post-offer inquiry about his/her condition or worker's compensation history.

An employer also may submit medical information and records concerning employees and applicants (obtained after a conditional job offer) to state workers' compensation offices and "second injury" funds without violating ADA confidentiality requirements.

Q. What is discrimination based on "relationship or association" under the ADA?

A. The ADA prohibits discrimination based on relationship or association in order to protect individuals from actions based on unfounded assumptions that their relationship to a person with a disability would affect their job performance, and from actions caused by bias or misinformation concerning certain disabilities. For example, this provision would protect a person whose spouse has a disability from being denied employment because of an employer's unfounded assumption that the applicant would use excessive leave to care for the spouse. It also would protect an individual who does volunteer work for people with AIDS from a discriminatory employment action motivated by that relationship or association.

Q. How are the employment provisions enforced?

A. The employment provisions of the ADA are enforced under the same procedures now applicable to race, color, sex, national origin, and religious discrimination under title VII of the Civil Rights Act of 1964, as amended, and the Civil Rights Act of 1991. Complaints regarding actions that occurred on or after July 26, 1992, may be filed with the Equal Employment Opportunity Commission or designated State human rights agencies. Available remedies will include hiring, reinstatement, promotion, back pay, front pay, restored benefits, reasonable accommodation, attorneys' fees, expert witness fees, and court costs. Compensatory and punitive damages also may be available in cases of intentional discrimination or where an employer fails to make a good faith effort to provide a reasonable accommodation.

Q.   What financial assistance is available to employers to help them make reasonable accommodations and comply with the ADA?

A.   A special tax credit is available to help smaller employers make accommodations required by the ADA. An eligible small business may take a tax credit of up to $5,000 per year for accommodations made to comply with the ADA. The credit is available for one-half the cost of "eligible access expenditures" that are more than $250 but less than $10,250.

A full tax deduction, up to $15,000 per year, also is available to any business for expenses of removing qualified architectural or transportation barriers. Expenses covered include costs of removing barriers created by steps, narrow doors, inaccessible parking spaces, restroom facilities, and transportation vehicles. Information about the tax credit and the tax deduction can be obtained from a local IRS office, or by contacting the Office of Chief Counsel, Internal Revenue Service.

Tax credits are available under the Targeted Jobs Tax Credit Program (TJTCP) for employers who hire individuals with disabilities referred by State or local vocational rehabilitation agencies, State Commissions on the Blind, or the U.S. Department of Veterans Affairs, and certified by a State Employment Service. Under the TJTCP, a tax credit may be taken for up to 40 percent of the first $6,000 of first-year wages of a new employee with a disability. This program must be reauthorized each year by Congress, and currently is extended through June 30, 1993. Further information about the TJTCP can be obtained from the State Employment Services or from State Governors' Committees on the Employment of People with Disabilities. [The program was not reauthorized in 1994.]

Q.   What are an employer's recordkeeping requirements under the employment provisions of the ADA?

A.   An employer must maintain records such as application forms submitted by applicants and other records related to hiring, requests for reasonable accommodation, promotion, demotion, transfer, lay-off or termination, rates of pay or other terms of compensation, and selection for training or apprenticeship for one year after making the record or taking the action described (whichever occurs later). If a charge of discrimination is filed or an action is brought by EEOC, an employer must save all personnel records related to the charge until final disposition of the charge.

Q.   Does the ADA require that an employer post a notice explaining its requirements?

A.   The ADA requires that employers post a notice describing the provisions of the ADA. It must be made accessible, as needed, to individuals with disabilities. A poster is available from EEOC summarizing the requirements of the ADA and other Federal legal requirements for nondiscrimination for which EEOC has enforcement responsibility. EEOC also provides guidance on making this information available in accessible formats for people with disabilities.

Q. What resources does the Equal Employment Opportunity Commission have available to help employers and people with disabilities understand and comply with the employment requirements of the ADA?

A. The Equal Employment Opportunity Commission has developed several resources to help employers and people with disabilities understand and comply with the employment provisions of the ADA.
Resources include:

■ A Technical Manual that provides "how-to" guidance on the employment provisions of the ADA as well as a resource directory to help individuals find specific information.

■ A variety of brochures, booklets, and fact sheets.

State and Local Governments

Q. Does the ADA apply to State and local governments?

A. Title II of the ADA prohibits discrimination against qualified individuals with disabilities in all programs, activities, and services of public entities. It applies to all State and local governments, their departments and agencies, and any other instrumentalities or special purpose districts of State or local governments. It clarifies the requirements of section 504 of the Rehabilitation Act of 1973 for public transportation systems that receive Federal financial assistance, and extends coverage to all public entities that provide public transportation, whether or not they receive Federal financial assistance. It establishes detailed standards for the operation of public transit systems, including commuter and intercity rail (AMTRAK).

Q. When do the requirements for State and local governments become effective?

A. In general, they became effective on January 26, 1992.

Q. How does title II affect participation in a State or local government's programs, activities, and services?

A. A state or local government must eliminate any eligibility criteria for participation in programs, activities, and services that screen out or tend to screen out persons with disabilities, unless it can establish that the requirements are necessary for the provision of the service, program, or activity. The State or local government may, however, adopt legitimate safety requirements necessary for safe operation if they are based on real risks, not on stereotypes or generalizations about individuals with disabilities. Finally, a public entity must reasonably modify its policies, practices, or procedures to avoid discrimination. If the public entity can demonstrate that a particular modification would fundamentally alter the nature of its service, program, or activity, it is not required to make that modification.

Q. Does title II cover a public entity's employment policies and practices?

A. Yes. Title II prohibits all public entities, regardless of the size of their workforce, from discriminating in employment against qualified individuals with disabilities. In addition to title II's employment coverage, title I of the ADA and section 504 of the Rehabilitation Act of 1973 prohibit employment discrimination against qualified individuals with disabilities by certain public entities.

Q. What changes must a public entity make to its existing facilities to make them accessible?

A. A public entity must ensure that individuals with disabilities are not excluded from services, programs, and activities because existing buildings are inaccessible. A State or local government's programs, when viewed in their entirety, must be readily accessible to and usable by individuals with disabilities. This standard, known as "program accessibility," applies to facilities of a public entity that existed on January 26, 1992. Public entities do not necessarily have to make each of their existing facilities accessible. They may provide program accessibility by a number of methods including alteration of existing facilities, acquisition or construction of additional facilities, relocation of a service or program to an accessible facility, or provision of services at alternate accessible sites.

Q. When must structural changes be made to attain program accessibility?

A. Structural changes needed for program accessibility must be made as expeditiously as possible, but no later than January 26, 1995. This three-year time period is not a grace period; all alterations must be accomplished as expeditiously as possible. A public entity that employs 50 or more persons must have developed a transition plan by July 26, 1992, setting forth the steps necessary to complete such changes.

Q. What is a self-evaluation?

A. A self-evaluation is a public entity's assessment of its current policies and practices. The self-evaluation identifies and corrects those policies and practices that are inconsistent with title II's requirements. All public entities must complete a self-evaluation by January 26, 1993. A public entity that employs 50 or more employees must retain its self-evaluation for three years. Other public entities are not required to retain their self-evaluations, but are encouraged to do so because these documents evidence a public entity's good faith efforts to comply with title II's requirements.

Q. What does title II require for new construction and alterations?

A. The ADA requires that all new buildings constructed by a State or local government be accessible. In addition, when a State or local government undertakes alterations to a building, it must make the altered portions accessible.

Q. How will a State or local government know that a new building is accessible?

A. A State or local government will be in compliance with the ADA for new construction and alterations if it follows either of two accessibility standards. It can chose either the Uniform Federal Accessibility Standards or the Americans with Disabilities Act Accessibility Guidelines for Buildings and Facilities, which is the standard that must be used for public accommodations and commercial facilities under title III of the ADA. If the State or local government chooses the ADA Accessibility Guidelines, it is not entitled to the elevator exemption (which permits certain private buildings under three stories or under 3,000 square feet per floor to be constructed without an elevator).

Q. What requirements apply to a public entity's emergency telephone services, such as 911?

A. State and local agencies that provide emergency telephone services must provide "direct access" to individuals who rely on a TDD or computer modem for telephone communication. Telephone access through a third party or through a relay service does not satisfy the requirement for direct access. Where a public entity provides 911 telephone service, it may not substitute a separate seven-digit telephone line as the sole means for access to 911 services by nonvoice users. A public entity may, however, provide a separate seven-digit line for the exclusive use of nonvoice callers in addition to providing direct access for such calls to its 911 line.

Q. Does title II require that telephone emergency service systems be compatible with all formats used for nonvoice communications?

A. No. At present, telephone emergency services must only be compatible with the Baudot format. Until it can be technically proven that communications in another format can operate in a reliable and compatible manner in a given telephone emergency environment, a public entity would not be required to provide direct access to computer modems using formats other than Baudot.

Q. How will the ADA's requirements for State and local governments be enforced?

A. Private individuals may bring lawsuits to enforce their rights under title II and may receive the same remedies as those provided under section 504 of the Rehabilitation Act of 1973, including reasonable attorney's fees. Individuals may also file complaints with eight designated Federal agencies, including the Department of Justice and the Department of Transportation.

Public Accommodations

Q. What are public accommodations?

A. A public accommodation is a private entity that owns, operates, leases, or leases to, a place of public accommodation. Places of public accommodation include a wide range of entities, such as restaurants, hotels, theaters, doctors' offices, pharmacies, retail stores, museums, libraries, parks, private schools, and day care centers. Private clubs and religious organizations are exempt from the ADA's title III requirements for public accommodations.

Q. Will the ADA have any effect on the eligibility criteria used by public accommodations to determine who may receive services?

A. Yes. If a criterion screens out or tends to screen out individuals with disabilities, it may only be used if necessary for the provision of the services. For instance, it would be a violation for a retail store to have a rule excluding all deaf persons from entering the premises, or for a movie theater to exclude all individuals with cerebral palsy. More subtle forms of discrimination are also prohibited. For example, requiring presentation of a driver's license as the sole acceptable means of identification for purposes of paying by check could constitute discrimination against individuals with vision impairments. This would be true if such individuals are ineligible to receive licenses and the use of an alternative means of identification is feasible.

Q. Does the ADA allow public accommodations to take safety factors into consideration in providing services to individuals with disabilities?

A. The ADA expressly provides that a public accommodation may exclude an individual, if that individual poses a direct threat to the health or safety of others that cannot be mitigated by appropriate modifications in the public accommodation's policies or procedures, or by the provision of auxiliary aids. A public accommodation will be permitted to establish objective safety criteria for the operation of its business; however, any safety standard must be based on objective requirements rather than stereotypes or generalizations about the ability of persons with disabilities to participate in an activity.

Q. Are there any limits on the kinds of modifications in policies, practices, and procedures required by the ADA?

A. Yes. The ADA does not require modifications that would fundamentally alter the nature of the services provided by the public accommodation. For example, it would not be discriminatory for a physician specialist who treats only burn patients to refer a deaf individual to another physician for treatment of a broken limb or respiratory ailment. To require a physician to accept patients outside of his or her specialty would fundamentally alter the nature of the medical practice.

Q. What kinds of auxiliary aids and services are required by the ADA to ensure effective communication with individuals with hearing or vision impairments?

A. Appropriate auxiliary aids and services may include services and devices such as qualified interpreters, assistive listening devices, notetakers, and written materials for individuals with hearing impairments; and qualified readers, taped texts, and brailled or large-print materials for individuals with vision impairments.

Q.   **Are there any limitations on the ADA's auxiliary aids requirements?**

A.   Yes. The ADA does not require the provision of any auxiliary aid that would result in an undue burden or in a fundamental alteration in the nature of the goods or services provided by a public accommodation. However, the public accommodation is not relieved from the duty to furnish an alternative auxiliary aid, if available, that would not result in a fundamental alteration or undue burden. Both of these limitations are derived from existing regulations and case law under section 504 of the Rehabilitation Act and are to be determined on a case-by-case basis.

Q.   **Will restaurants be required to have brailled menus?**

A.   No, not if waiters or other employees are made available to read the menu to a blind customer.

Q.   **Will a clothing store be required to have brailled price tags?**

A.   No, not if sales personnel could provide price information orally upon request.

Q.   **Will a bookstore be required to maintain a sign language interpreter on its staff in order to communicate with deaf customers?**

A.   No, not if employees communicate by pen and notepad when necessary.

Q.   **Are there any limitations on the ADA's barrier removal requirements for existing facilities?**

A.   Yes. Barrier removal need be accomplished only when it is "readily achievable" to do so.

Q.   **What does the term "readily achievable" mean?**

A.   It means "easily accomplishable and able to be carried out without much difficulty or expense."

Q.   **What are examples of the types of modifications that would be readily achievable in most cases?**

A.   Examples include the simple ramping of a few steps, the installation of grab bars where only routine reinforcement of the wall is required, the lowering of telephones, and similar modest adjustments.

Q.   **Will businesses need to arrange furniture and display racks?**

A.   Possibly. For example, restaurants may need to rearrange tables and department stores may need to adjust their layout of racks and shelves in order to permit access to wheelchair users.

Q.   **Will businesses need to install elevators?**

A.   Businesses are not required to retrofit their facilities to install elevators unless such installation is readily achievable, which is unlikely in most cases.

Q. When barrier removal is not readily achievable, what kinds of alternative steps are required by the ADA?

A. Alternatives may include such measures as in-store assistance for removing articles from inaccessible shelves, home delivery of groceries, or coming to the door to receive or return dry cleaning.

Q. Must alternative steps be taken without regard to cost?

A. No, only readily achievable alternative steps must be undertaken.

Q. How is "readily achievable" determined in a multisite business?

A. In determining whether an action to make a public accommodation accessible would be "readily achievable," the overall size of the parent corporation or entity is only one factor to be considered. The ADA also permits consideration of the financial resources of the particular facility or facilities involved and the administrative or fiscal relationship of the facility or facilities to the parent entity.

Q. Who has responsibility for ADA compliance in leased places of public accommodation, the landlord or the tenant?

A. The ADA places the legal obligation to remove barriers or provide auxiliary aids and services on both the landlord and the tenant. The landlord and the tenant may decide by lease who will actually make the changes and provide the aids and services, but both remain legally responsible.

Q. What does the ADA require in new construction?

A. The ADA requires that all new construction of places of public accommodation, as well as of "commercial facilities" such as office buildings, be accessible. Elevators are generally not required in facilities under three stories or with fewer than 3,000 square feet per floor, unless the building is a shopping center or mall; the professional office of a health care provider; a terminal, depot, or other public transit station; or an airport passenger terminal.

Q. Is it expensive to make all newly constructed places of public accommodation and commercial facilities accessible?

A. The cost of incorporating accessibility features in new construction is less than one percent of construction costs. This is a small price in relation to the economic benefits to be derived from full accessibility in the future, such as increased employment and consumer spending and decreased welfare dependency.

Q. Must every feature of a new facility be accessible?

A. No, only a specified number of elements such as parking spaces and drinking fountains must be made accessible in order for a facility to be "readily accessible." Certain nonoccupiable spaces such as elevator pits, elevator penthouses, and piping or equipment catwalks need not be accessible.

Q. What are the ADA requirements for altering facilities?

A. All alterations that could affect the usability of a facility must be made in an accessible manner to the maximum extent feasible. For example, if during renovations a doorway is being relocated, the new doorway must be wide enough to meet the new construction standard for accessibility. When alterations are made to a primary function area, such as the lobby of a bank or the dining area of a cafeteria, an accessible path of travel to the altered area must also be provided. The bathrooms, telephones, and drinking fountains serving that area must also be made accessible. These additional accessibility alterations are only required to the extent that the added accessibility costs do not exceed 20 percent of the cost of the original alteration. Elevators are generally not required in facilities under three stories or with fewer than 3,000 square feet per floor, unless the building is a shopping center or mall; the professional office of a health care provider; a terminal, depot, or other public transit station; or an airport passenger terminal.

Q. Does the ADA permit an individual with a disability to sue a business when that individual believes that discrimination is about to occur, or must the individual wait for the discrimination to occur?

A. The ADA public accommodations provisions permit an individual to allege discrimination based on a reasonable belief that discrimination is about to occur. This provision, for example, allows a person who uses a wheelchair to challenge the planned construction of a new place of public accommodation, such as a shopping mall, that would not be accessible to individuals who use wheelchairs. The resolution of such challenges prior to the construction of an inaccessible facility would enable any necessary remedial measures to be incorporated in the building at the planning stage, when such changes would be relatively inexpensive.

Q. How does the ADA affect existing State and local building codes?

A. Existing codes remain in effect. The ADA allows the Attorney General to certify that a State law, local building code, or similar ordinance that establishes accessibility requirements meets or exceeds the minimum accessibility requirements for public accommodations and commercial facilities. Any State or local government may apply for certification of its code or ordinance. The Attorney General can certify a code or ordinance only after prior notice and a public hearing at which interested people, including individuals with disabilities, are provided an opportunity to testify against the certification.

Q. What is the effect of certification of a State or local code or ordinance?

A. Certification can be advantageous if an entity has constructed or altered a facility according to a certified code or ordinance. If someone later brings an enforcement proceeding against the entity, the certification is considered "rebuttable evidence" that the State law or local ordinance meets or exceeds the minimum requirements of the ADA. In other words, the entity can argue that the construction or alteration met the requirements of the

ADA because it was done in compliance with the State or local code that had been certified.

Q. **When are the public accommodations provisions effective?**

A. In general, they became effective on January 26, 1992.

Q. **How will the public accommodations provisions be enforced?**

A. Private individuals may bring lawsuits in which they can obtain court orders to stop discrimination. Individuals may also file complaints with the Attorney General, who is authorized to bring lawsuits in cases of general public importance or where a "pattern or practice" of discrimination is alleged. In these cases, the Attorney General may seek monetary damages and civil penalties. Civil penalties may not exceed $50,000 for a first violation or $100,000 for any subsequent violation.

Miscellaneous

Q. **Is the Federal government covered by the ADA?**

A. The ADA does not cover the executive branch of the Federal government. The executive branch continues to be covered by title V of the Rehabilitation Act of 1973, which prohibits discrimination in services and employment on the basis of handicap and which is a model for the requirements of the ADA. The ADA, however, does cover Congress and other entities in the legislative branch of the Federal government.

Q. **Does the ADA cover private apartments and private homes?**

A. The ADA does not cover strictly residential private apartments and homes. If, however, a place of public accommodation, such as a doctor's office or day care center, is located in a private residence, those portions of the residence used for that purpose are subject to the ADA's requirements.

Q. **Does the ADA cover air transportation?**

A. Discrimination by air carriers in areas other than employment is not covered by the ADA but rather by the Air Carrier Access Act (49 U.S.C. 1374 (c)).

Q. **What are the ADA's requirements for public transit buses?**

A. The Department of Transportation has issued regulations mandating accessible public transit vehicles and facilities. The regulations include requirements that all new fixed-route, public transit buses be accessible and that supplementary paratransit services be provided for those individuals with disabilities who cannot use fixed-route bus service.

Q. **How will the ADA make telecommunications accessible?**

A. The ADA requires the establishment of telephone relay services for individuals who use telecommunications devices for deaf persons (TDDs) or similar devices. The Federal Communications Commission has issued regulations specifying standards for the operation of these services.

Q. Are businesses entitled to any tax benefit to help pay for the cost of compliance?

A. As amended in 1990, the Internal Revenue Code allows a deduction of up to $15,000 per year for expenses associated with the removal of qualified architectural and transportation barriers.

The 1990 amendment also permits eligible small businesses to receive a tax credit for certain costs of compliance with the ADA. An eligible small business is one whose gross receipts do not exceed $1,000,000 or whose workforce does not consist of more than 30 full-time workers. Qualifying businesses may claim a credit of up to 50 percent of eligible access expenditures that exceed $250 but do not exceed $10,250. Examples of eligible access expenditures include the necessary and reasonable costs of removing architectural, physical, communications, and transportation barriers; providing readers, interpreters, and other auxiliary aids; and acquiring or modifying equipment or devices.

Resources

Telephone Numbers for ADA Information

This list contains the telephone numbers of Federal agencies that are responsible for providing information to the public about the Americans with Disabilities Act and organizations that have been funded by the Federal government to provide information through staffed information centers.

The agencies and organizations listed are sources for obtaining information about the law's requirements and informal guidance in understanding and complying with the ADA. They are not, and should not be viewed as, sources for obtaining legal advice or legal opinions about your rights or responsibilities under the ADA.

Architectural and Transportation Barriers Compliance Board
800-872-2253 (voice & TDD)

Equal Employment Opportunity Commission
For questions and documents
800-669-3362 (voice)   800-800-3302 (TDD)

Alternate number for ordering documents (print and other formats)
202-663-4264 (voice)   202-663-7110 (TDD)

Federal Communications Commission

For ADA documents and general information
202-632-7260 (voice)   202-632-6999 (TDD)

Job Accommodation Network
800-526-7234 (voice)   800-526-7234 (TDD)

Within West Virginia
800-526-4698 (voice & TDD)

President's Committee on Employment of People with Disabilities
Information Line: ADA Work
 800-232-9675 (voice & TDD)

Rural Transit Assistance Program (for information and assistance on public transportation issues)
 800-527-8279 (voice & TDD)

U.S. Department of Justice
 202-514-0301 (voice) 202-514-0383 (TDD)

U.S. Department of Transportation

 Federal Transit Administration (for ADA documents and information)
  202-366-1656 (voice) 202-366-2979 (TDD)

 Office of the General Counsel (for legal questions)
  202-366-9306 (voice) 207-755-7687 (TDD)

 Federal Aviation Administration
  202-376-6406 (voice)

Regional Disability and Business Technical Assistance Centers

ADA information, assistance, and copies of ADA documents supplied by the Equal Employment Opportunity Commission and the Department of Justice, which are available in standard print, large print, audio cassette, braille, and computer disk, may be obtained from any of the ten Regional Disability and Business Technical Assistance Centers.

Toll-free number for reaching any of the following Centers
 800-949-4232 (voice & TDD)

Region I
(Maine, New Hampshire, Vermont, Massachusetts, Rhode Island, Connecticut)
 207-874-6535 (voice & TDD)

Region II
(New York, New Jersey, Puerto Rico)
 609-392-4004 (voice) 609-392-7004 (TDD)

Region III
(Pennsylvania, Delaware, Maryland, District of Columbia, Virginia, West Virginia)
 703-525-3268 (voice & TDD)

Region IV
(Kentucky, Tennessee, North Carolina, South Carolina, Georgia, Alabama, Mississippi, Florida)
 404-888-0022 (voice) 404-888-9098 (TDD)

Region V
(Ohio, Indiana, Illinois, Michigan, Wisconsin, Minnesota)
312-413-7756 (voice & TDD)

Region VI
(Arkansas, Louisiana, Oklahoma, Texas, New Mexico)
713-520-0232 (voice)   713-520-5136 (TDD)

Region VII
(Iowa, Missouri, Nebraska, Kansas)
314-882-3600 (voice & TDD)

Region VIII
(North Dakota, South Dakota, Montana, Wyoming, Colorado, Utah)
719-444-0252 (voice & TDD)

Region IX
(Arizona, Nevada, California, Hawaii, Pacific Basin)
510-465-7884 (voice)   510-465-3172 (TDD)

Region X
(Idaho, Oregon, Washington, Alaska)
206-438-3168 (voice)   206-438-3167 (TDD)

Addresses for ADA Information

Architectural and Transportation Barriers
Compliance Board
1331 F Street NW
Suite 1000
Washington, DC 20004-1111

Federal Communications Commission
1919 M Street NW
Washington, DC 20554

U.S. Department of Justice
Civil Rights Division
Public Access Section
P.O. Box 66738
Washington, DC 20035-6738

U.S. Department of Transportation
400 Seventh Street SW
Washington, DC 20590

U.S. Equal Employment Opportunity Commission
1801 L Street NW
Washington, DC 20507

- Braille
- Large print
- Audiocassette
- Electronic file on computer disk and electronic bulletin board 202-514-6193

APPENDIX C
Adaptive Technology Exhibitors

Deaf Action Center of Greater New Orleans
1231 Prytania St.
New Orleans, LA 70130
504-525-7911
Fax 504-525-9826
Lisa Haydel
TDD Coordinator
Assistive devices for the deaf
and hearing-impaired

Gaylord Bros.
7272 Morgan Road
Liverpool, NY 13090
800-448-6160
Fax 800-272-3412
Spencer Rhoads
Sr. Product Manager/Furniture
Reading assistive items
ADA-related door openers

Highsmith Company
W. 5527 Highway 106E
P.O. Box 800
Fort Atkinson, WI 53538
414-563-9571
Barbara Endl
200 catalogs
11x17 poster

Innoventions, Inc.
5921 S. Middlefield Road
Suite 102
Littleton, CO 80123-2877
303-797-6554
800-854-6554
Fax 303-797-1320
Edward R. Bettinardi
President
Magni-Cam electronic magnifier

Phonic Ear, Inc.
3880 Cypress Drive
Petaluma, CA 94954-7600
707-769-1110
800-227-0735
Fax 707-769-9624
Herb Dixon
Regional Sales Manager
FM hearing systems

TeleSensory
455 N. Bernardo Ave.
P.O. Box 7455
Mountain View, CA 94039-7455
415-960-0920
Marc Stenzel
Director of National Account Sales
TeleSensory products
Computer system for enlarging print
Closed-circuit TV for enlarging print

University Copy Services, Inc.
2405 Bond St.
University Park, IL 60466
800-762-2736
John Franzese
President
Selectec book monitor copier

WGBH Accessible Media
WGBH Educational Foundation
125 Western Ave.
Boston, MA 02134
617-492-2777
Sharon King and Mary Ann Pack
Videos and tapes
Packets explaining information
Brochures explaining home video catalogs

Selected Bibliography

compiled by Barbara T. Mates

Handbooks, Manuals, Bibliographies

ADA Bibliography. Salt Lake City: Utah State Library Division, 1993.

ADA Compliance Guide: Americans with Disabilities Act. Washington, D.C.: Thompson, 1990.

ADA Resource Notebook for Public Libraries: The Americans with Disabilities Act: A Challenge and an Opportunity. Watertown, Mass.: The Library, 1993.

ADA Training Manual for Managers and Supervisors: A Guide to Americans with Disabilities Act Compliance. Chicago: Commerce Clearing House, 1992.

American Disability Act. Indianapolis: Indiana Continuing Legal Education Forum, 1991.

Americans with Disabilities Act: A Practical and Legal Guide to Impact, Enforcement, and Compliance. A BNA Special Report. Washington, D.C.: Bureau of National Affairs, 1990.

Americans with Disabilities Act: Facilities Compliance Workbook. New York: Wiley, 1992.

Americans with Disabilities Act of 1990: Selected Regulations. Chicago: Commerce Clearing House, 1991.

Analysis of the Americans with Disabilities Act and the EEOC Regulations. New York: Research Institute of America, 1991.

Complying with the Americans with Disabilities Act of 1990. Rev. ed. Washington, D.C.: National League of Cities, 1991.

Crispen, Joanne L., ed. *The Americans with Disabilities Act: Its Impact on Libraries: The Library's Responses in "Doable" Steps*. Chicago: American Library Association, ASCLA, 1993.

Fersch, Don and Peter W. Thomas. *Complying with the Americans with Disabilities Act: A Guidebook for Management and People with Disabilities*. Westport, Conn.: Quorum Books, 1993.

Frierson, James G. *Employer's Guide to the Americans with Disabilities Act*. Washington, D.C.: Bureau of National Affairs, 1992.

Handicapped Requirements Handbook. Washington, D.C.: Federal Programs Advisory Service, 1990.

Harrison, Maureen and Steve Gilbert, eds. *The Americans with Disabilities Act Handbook*. Beverly Hills, Calif.: Excellent Books, 1992.

Quirk, William J. *New Hiring, Promotion, and Termination Rules for the 1990's: New Rules Dealing with the Disabled, Older Workers, and Women*. New York: Panel Publishers for Institute for Management, 1991.

U.S. Architectural and Transportation Barriers Compliance Board. *Americans with Disabilities Act (ADA): Accessibility Guidelines for Buildings and Facilities, Transportation Facilities, Transportation Vehicles*. Washington, D.C.: U.S. Access Board, 1994.

Application of the ADA

Accessibility and Historic Preservation: Resource Guide. Windsor, Vt.: Historic Windsor, 1993.

"ADA: A Special Issue." *Worklife* 3 (Fall 1990): 1–48.

"ADA Do's and Don'ts." *Management Review* 81 (August 1992): 7.

"ADA: Employment Rights." *Paraplegia News* 45 (November 1991): 27–29.

The ADA: Mandate for Social Change. Baltimore: P. H. Books, 1993.

"Adaptive Libraries: Technology and Services." *Computers in Libraries* 12 (December 1992): 77–78.

The Americans with Disabilities Act: A Review of Best Practices. New York: AMA Membership Management Association, 1993.

Americans with Disabilities Act: Employee Rights and Employer Obligations. Oakland, Calif.: Matthew Bender, 1992.

Americans with Disabilities Act: From Policy to Practice. New York: Milbank Memorial Fund, 1991.

The Americans with Disabilities Act (ADA), Libraries and the Law; Educational Seminar of the Social Law Library. Boston: Proprietors of the Social Law Library, 1993.

Balas, Janet. "Online Disability Information." *Computers in Libraries* 12 (November 1992): 26–31.

Baldwin Public Library's Policies in Compliance with the Americans with Disabilities Act. Birmingham, Mich.: The Library, 1993.

Black, J. B., et al. *Surveying Public Libraries for the ADA*. Tallahassee, Fla.: Bureau of Library Development, Division of Library and Information Services, 1992.

BOMA International's ADA Compliance Guidebook: A Checklist for Your Building: Meeting Title III Provisions of the Americans with Disabilities Act: Public Accommodations and Commercial Facilities. Washington, D.C.: BOMA International, 1992.

Bosco, Pearl. "ADA: Finding Order in the Law." *Buildings* 87 (January 1993): 37–38.

Brown, Carl. "Assistive Technology Computers and Persons with Disabilities." *Communications of the ACM* 35 (May 1992): 36–45.

Cassell, Marianne Koch and the Vermont Board of Libraries Access Task Force. *Planning for Accessibility*. Montpelier, Vt.: Department of Libraries, 1991.

Chase, Anne. "Coping with the Disabilities Act." *Governing* 5 (August 1992): 18–19.

Communication Access for Persons with Hearing Loss: Compliance with the Americans with Disabilities Act (ADA). Baltimore: York Pr., 1994.

Cross, Evelina W. "Implementing the Americans with Disabilities Act." *Journal of the American Dietetic Association* 93 (March 1993): 273–275.

Dalton, Phyllis L. *Library Services to the Deaf and Hearing Impaired*. Phoenix, Ariz.: Oryx, 1985.

———. "Productivity Not Paternalism." *Library Personnel News* 4 (Summer 1990): 42–43.

Davies, Daniel K. and Randy W. Dipner. "ACM Membership Survey of Disability and Disability Issues." *Communications of the ACM* 35 (May 1992): 91–93.

Dipner, Randy W. "ADA and the ACM." *Communications of the ACM* 35 (May 1992): 89–90.

Drach, Richard. "Making Reasonable Accommodations under the ADA." *Employment Relations Today* 19 (Summer 1992): 167–175.

Duston, Robert Lewis. *A Guide to Writing Job Descriptions under the Americans with Disabilities Act*. Washington, D.C.: College and University Personnel Association, 1992.

Esposito, Michael D. "Are You 100 Percent ADA-Compliant?" *Management Review* 82 (February 1992): 27–29.

Foos, Donald D. and Nancy C. Pack, eds. *How Libraries Must Comply with the Americans with Disabilities Act (ADA)*. Phoenix, Ariz.: Oryx, 1992.

Foster, Terry and Linda Lindell. "Libraries and the Americans with Disabilities Act." *Texas Libraries* 52 (Fall 1991): 59–63.

Fyock, Catherine D. *Employing People with Capabilities: Responding to the Americans with Disabilities Act: Module I of the Managing Diversity Series*. Burr Ridge, Ill.: Irwin, 1994.

Goldman, Warren R. and James R. Mallory. "Overcoming Communication Barriers: Communicating with Deaf People." *Library Trends* 41 (Summer 1992): 21–30.

Hayden, Mary Jean. "Disability Awareness Workshop: Helping Business Comply with the Americans with Disabilities Act." *American Journal of Occupational Therapy* 46 (May 1992): 461–465.

"How to Comply with the Americans with Disabilities Act." *Business and Health* 10 (August 1992): 45.

"Implementing the Americans with Disabilities Act of 1990: Assessing the Variables of Success." *Public Administration Review* 53 (March 1993): 121–128.

Jaben, Jan. "Enabling the Disabled: IBM, Xerox, AT&T Market New Products to Aid People with Disabilities." *Business Marketing* 77 (July 1992): 24.

Karp, Rashelle S. *Library Services for Disabled Individuals*. Boston: G. K. Hall, 1991.

Koening, Dennis. "Look on the Disabilities Act as an Opportunity Rather than a Burden." *InfoWorld* 14 (November 23, 1992): 39.

Kovalik, Gail L. "'Silent' Films Revisited: Captioned Films for the Deaf." *Library Trends* 41 (Summer 1992): 100–117.

Laurie, Ty D. "Libraries' Duties to Accommodate Their Patrons under the Americans with Disabilities Act." *Library Administration & Management* 6 (Fall 1992): 204–205.

Lazzaro, Joseph J. *Adaptive Technologies for Learning and Work Environments*. Chicago: American Library Association, 1993.

Lewis, Christopher. "Americans with Disabilities Act and Its Effect on Public Libraries." *Public Libraries* 32 (January/February 1992): 23–28.

Library Services for People with Disabilities. 3 v. Tallahassee: Florida State Library, Bureau of Library Development, 1991.

Lord, Mary. "Away with Barriers: How to Comply with the Americans with Disabilities Act." *U.S. News & World Report* 113 (July 20, 1992): 60–63.

Mates, Barbara T. "Adaptive Technology Makes Libraries 'People Friendly.'" *Computers in Libraries* 12 (November 1992): 20–25.

———. "Adaptive Technology for the 90's." *Computers in Libraries* 13 (February 1993): 54–55.

Matthes, Karen. "Awareness Training: First-Hand Experience Working with Disabilities." *HR Focus* 1992 69 (July 1992): 19.

McCormick, Brian. "What Office Changes Are Required under Disabilities Act?" *American Medical News* 35 (November 9, 1992): 10.

McCormick, John A. *Computers and the Americans with Disabilities Act: A Manager's Guide*. New York: Windcrest, 1994.

McNulty, Tom. "Reference Services for Students with Disabilities: Desktop Braille Publishing in the Academic Library." *RSR* 21 (1993): 37–44.

Michaels, Andrea and David Michaels. "Designing for Technology in Today's Libraries." *Computers in Libraries* 12 (November 1992): 8–10+.

Minton, Eric. "Plunging into the Mainstream." *Planning* 58 (August 1992): 18.

Mishkin, Douglas B. and Eric S. Shuster. "Understanding the ADA." *Association Management* 43 (April 1991): 51–54.

Pack, Nancy C. and Donald Dale Foos. "Library Compliance with the Americans with Disabilities Act." *RQ* 32 (Winter 1992): 255–267.

Pati, Gopal. "The Disabled Are Able to Work." *Personnel Journal* 69 (December 1990): 30–32.

People with Disabilities Explain It All for You: Your Guide to the Public Accommodations Requirements of the Americans with Disabilities Act. Louisville, Ky.: Avocado Pr., 1992.

Pimentel, Richard. *What Managers and Supervisors Need to Know about the ADA*. San Francisco: Milt Wright, 1992.

The Red Notebook: Library and Information Services to the Deaf Community. Silver Springs, Md.: Library for Deaf Action, 1993.

Rettig, Marc. "A Succotash of Projections and Insights." *Communications of the ACM* 35 (May 1992): 25–31.

Roundtable for Libraries Serving Special Populations. "Guidelines for Libraries Serving Persons with a Hearing Impairment." *Library Trends* 41 (Summer 1992): 164–172.

Tavenner, Mary T. "The ADA: Changing the Way You Do Business." *Industrial Distribution* 81 (August 1992): 70.

"Toolkit for ADA." *Management Review* 82 (February 1993): 33–35.

Treanor, Richard Bryant. *We Overcame: The Story of Civil Rights for Disabled People*. Falls Church, Va.: Regal Direct, 1993.

U.S. General Accounting Office. *Americans with Disabilities Act: Initial Accessibility Good But Important Barriers Remain: Report to the Chairman, Subcommittee on Select Education and Civil Rights, Committee on Education and Labor, House of Representatives*. Washington, D.C.: GAO, 1993.

Velleman, Ruth A. *Meeting the Needs of People with Disabilities: A Guide for Librarians, Educators, and Other Service Professionals*. Phoenix, Ariz.: Oryx, 1990.

Vernon-Oehmke, Arlene. "Management Needs Understanding and Sensitivity." *HR Focus* 1992 69 (July 1992): 20.

Wakelee-Lynch, Joseph. "Know Your Rights." *Diabetes Forecast* 45 (June 1992): 64–66.

Wright, Kieth C. and Judith F. Davie. *The Library Manager's Guide to Hiring and Serving Disabled Persons*. Jefferson, N.C.: McFarland, 1990.

———. *Libraries and the Disabled: The Library Manager's Handbook*. New York: Greenwood, 1991.

———. *Serving the Disabled: A How-to-Do-It Manual for Librarians*. New York: Neal-Schuman, 1991.

Video Resources

AFB ADA Consulting Group. *Strategies for Community Access: Braille and Raised Large Print Facility Signs*. 6 min. New York: American Foundation for the Blind, 1991.

And Access for All: ADA and Your Library. 47 min. Townsend, Md.: Library Video Network, 1993.

And Justice for All. 57 min. Dunbar: West Virginia Research and Training Center, 1991.

Blind Enough to See. 28 min. Schaumburg, Ill.: Marx Advertising and Video Publishing, 1993.

A Challenge to America: The Americans with Disabilities Act. 36 min. [S.l.]: Program Development Associates, 1991.

Nobody Is Burning Wheelchairs. 18 min. Chicago: National Easter Seal Society, 1992.

People First: Serving and Employing People with Disabilities. 38 min. Townsend, Md.: Library Video Network, 1990.

A Place Where I Belong: Serving Disabled Children in the Library. 19 min. Vancouver: Greater Vancouver Library Assn. and the National Library of Canada, 1987.

They Just Want into Whatever's Going On: A Production in Support of the Summer Institute on Library Services for Youth with Disabilities. 20 min. Bloomington: Indiana Univ., Instructional Television and Special Projects, 1990.

A VideoGuide to (dis)Ability Awareness. 25 min. Boston: Fanlight Productions, 1993.

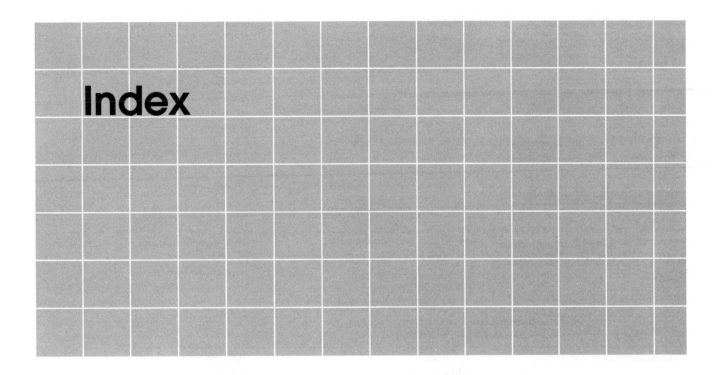

Index

ADA Accessibility Guidelines (ADAAG), 8
adaptive technology, 33–39. *See also* assistive devices
administration, 12
advisory committees, 4, 5, 6, 17, 51
affirmative action requirements, 69
age-related disabilities, 41
air transportation, 83
alarm systems, 11, 36, 56–57
alcoholics, 73
alterations, 21, 82
alternative methods of access for historic buildings, 21
Americans with Disabilities Act, 6–13, 66–87
areas of refuge, 15, 57
arthritis, 41
assistance, inappropriate, 4–5
assistive devices, 40–47, 42. *See also* adaptive technology
required by ADA, 79–80
attendance and leave policies, 72
attitudes, 3–5, 17
Audio-Link devices, 36
audits, accessibility, 16, 44, 54
auxiliary aids and services, 7–8, 10, 13. *See also* adaptive technology; assistive devices; Braille signage; TDD communications

back pain, 44
balance difficulties, 43
barrier removal, 80–81
Becker CPA Review, United States v., 10, 13
blind employees, 17
blind people, 3, 41, 49, 64. *See also* visually impaired people
alarms, 56, 60
protruding objects, 55
BOMA *International ADA Compliance Guidebook,* 16
book detection systems, 55–56
bookmobile services, 11–12
Braille access, 35, 80
Braille signage, 49
building codes, 12–13, 82–83
building design, 14–18, 59–61
Building Officials Conference of America (BOCA), 12–13

carpeting, 27
carrels, 31
carrying difficulties, 43
CCD. *See* closed circuit display
CCTV. *See* closed circuit television
clearance, 25–26, 31
closed captioned videos, 36
closed circuit display, 34
closed circuit television, 34

codes, building, 12–13, 82–83
colors of signage, 50
compact shelving, 64–65
companions, 42
compliance, levels of, 21

deaf employees, 17
deaf people, 41, 64, 80. *See also* hearing-impaired people
debilitating conditions, 41
design issues, 59–61
District of Columbia, Galloway v., 10, 13
dogs, assistance, 5, 42
domes, truncated, 60
"Don't Make Me Do It," (ADA section 501D) 1
doors, 63
drinking fountains, 16
drugs, illegal, 72–73

electric wires and cords, 44
elevators, 15, 80–81
emergency equipment, 42
emergency preparedness, 56–58
employee accommodation, 17
employment discrimination, 67
employment provisions of ADA, 6–7, 67
employment testing, 71
entrances, accessible, 59–60
epilepsy, light-induced, 56

Equal Employment Opportunity Commission, 7, 74–75, 76

federal buildings, 18, 83
financial assistance to employers, 75
fire protected areas, 15, 57
501 D, 1
floor surfaces, 27, 54–55, 60
fundamental alterations, 7–8
funding, 9
furnishing, adaptive, 45

Galloway v. the District of Columbia, 10, 13
glare, 50–51
grasping difficulties, 44

health and safety requirements, 72, 73
hearing-impaired people, 35–36, 41, 43, 56. See also deaf people
height of work surfaces, 26
historic buildings, 19–23
    minimum requirements, 21–22

International House of Pancakes, 10, 13
International Symbol of Accessibility, 48–49
Ivins, Molly, 19

job descriptions, 69

keyboard height, 44
keyboards, alternate, 34, 35
Kinney v. Yerusalem, 10, 13
knee space, 44

large print, 34
lavatories. See restrooms
lazy susans, 44
leased property, 12
Lewis, Gib, 19
lifting difficulties, 43
light switches, 15
lighting, 42
limitations, other, 41–42

maps, 50
mats, 63
medical examinations, 68
meeting rooms, 11
mirrors
    and deaf, 17
    and low bookshelves, 64

new construction, 81
911 telephone services, 78
noise, 42, 64
nonambulatory persons, 40–41

106 process, 22
optical character recognition (OCR), 35

pagers, vibrating, 17, 56
parking, 15, 59
paving materials, 15
Phonic Ear Easy-Listener FM Hearing Assistance System, 36
photo identification cards, 10
posting of requirements, 75–76
preferences, employment, 68
priorities for work to be done, 16–17
private accommodations, 83
private colleges, 12
program access provision of ADA, 7–8, 77
protruding objects, 55
Public Access Section, Department of Justice, 9
public accommodations, 78–83
public transportation, 83

qualified individuals with a disability, 67

ramps, 15, 53–54, 60
reaching ranges, 27–28, 43, 44
readily achievable measures, 80–81
reasonable accommodation, 7, 69–71
recently disabled people, 41
recordkeeping requirements, 75
Regional Disability and Business Technical Assistance Centers, 85–86
relationship or association protection, 74
rescue assistance, 15, 57
restrooms, 15, 60
retrofitting, 10–11, 15–16, 71, 77
routes to accessible seating, 26–27

safety and security considerations, 36, 53–58, 79
seating, 24–32
security equipment, 11
self-evaluation, 77
service desks, 60–61
SHPO. See State Historic Preservation Officer
signage, 31, 48–52
    Braille, 15
    emergency, 56–57

sitting difficulties, 42
Snell Library, Northeastern University, 28–32
Southern Building Congress, 12–13
specialized seating areas, 31
speech limitations, 41
stack access, 63–64
stairs, 60
state and local governments, 76–78
State Historic Preservation Officer, 20–21
storage, 42

tactile warnings, 55
tax credits and deductions, 75, 84
TDD communications, 9, 17, 35–36, 78, 83
telecommunications, 83
telecommunications device for the deaf. See TDD communications
telephone numbers for ADA information, 84–86
temporary buildings, 17
Title I, 66
Title II, 76–78
    and emergency preparedness, 54
Title III
    and emergency preparedness, 54
    and historic buildings, 19
trailers (temporary buildings), 17–18
training of staff, 57
TTY. See TDD communications

undue financial burdens, 11, 12
Uniform Federal Accessibility Standards (UFAS), 8, 54
United States v. Becker CPA Review, 10, 13
unskilled disabled, 41

vendors, 88–89
    adaptive furnishings, 46–47
    adaptive technology products, 36–39
visually impaired people, 4, 41, 43. See also blind people
voice output, 34–35

wheelchairs, 40–41, 44
    evacuation of, 15, 57
wheelchairs, motorized, 44, 55
windows, 15
work surfaces, 44
workers' compensation programs, 73–74

Yerusalem, Kinney v., 10, 13